DEVOTIONAL LIFE
IN THE WESLEYAN
TRADITION

DEVOTIONAL LIFE
IN THE WESLEYAN
TRADITION

A WORKBOOK

STEVE HARPER

UPPER
ROOM BOOKS®

Devotional Life in the Wesleyan Traditon: A Workbook
© 1995 by Steve Harper
All rights reserved.

The Upper Room® Web site http:/www.upperroom.org

Cover design and photograph: Steve Laughbaum
Interior design: Charles Sutherland
Eighth printing: 2008

Library of Congress Catalog Number: 95-60923
ISBN: 978-0-8358-0740-1
ISBN: 0-8358-0740-1

Printed in the United States of America

For Jeannie,
My wife, best friend, and spiritual guide

On the occasion of our
twenty-fifth year of marriage

CONTENTS

Introduction   9

Week One   19
John Wesley: Man of Devotion

Week Two   41
Constant Company with Christ

Week Three   61
The All-Sufficient Word

Week Four   79
Food for the Journey

Week Five   99
Hunger for Righteousness

Week Six   119
Life Together

Week Seven   141
Into the World

Introduction

Millions of people, longing for something more, are hungry for God. This hunger is as evident in the church as it is in the culture. Christians are tired of playing church and believe that the time has come to either get with it or get out. The desire for solid, spiritual formation is greater now than at any other period in my lifetime. Institutional religion has proven itself impotent to give abundant life. We must have something more.

We are people of the Book. We take our cues and receive our marching orders from scripture. We believe God speaks the ultimate word (revelation) and we respond. We are not interested in a spirituality foreign to or isolated from the Bible. At the same time, however, we believe God has spoken through tradition. We believe the great cloud of witnesses is filled with saints whose lives and teachings illumine our path and help us interpret the Book as we apply its timeless truths to ourselves and our situation.

One such person is John Wesley. By examining his life and ministry we can uncover rich, practical ideas for strengthening our devotional lives. This workbook is designed to provide you with personal enrichment as you use Wesley as a window through whom to view the spiritual life. If you stop with him, you will miss the point. If you pass through him into Christ, you will be blessed. If you use him as a guru, you will be disappointed. If you use him as a guide, you will be delighted.

If Wesley could say anything about the spiritual life to contemporary Christians, it might well be, "God does not call you to have a devotional time; God calls you to live a devotional life." A look at his massive writings reveals that, for him, the devotional life was much more related to the entirety of his experiences than to specific prayer times. Without question Wesley observed fixed times of devotion—and did so for more than sixty years! But to define his spiritual life by those times alone would miss the full picture of his spirituality. For him, every moment was a God moment, an occasion for God to reveal and for him to respond. As you begin this workbook, you will have many moments in which to reflect personally and deeply on your spiritual life.

A word of caution: One of the greatest dangers in contemporary spiritual formation is the temptation to turn it into another program. We are so good at this in the church. But if we attempt to make the spiritual life an event, it will die. And it should. For we will have reduced the life of God in the human soul to rules and regulations, fads and emphases, lists and techniques. We will have forgotten the key thing Wesley would want us to remember: the spiritual life is not a part of life, it is life.

So use this workbook as a means, not an end. Use it as an opportunity, not as a compartment. Use it as an avenue of grace, not a measurement of maturity. Only then will you know devotional life in the Wesleyan tradition.

The Formative Process

Spiritual formation cannot be programmed, but it can be directed. This workbook is designed to encourage and facilitate a formative experience for you. It is contemporary in format, yet related to ancient practices that have proven their value. Each day will follow a fourfold path of reading, reflecting, recording, and relating.

You will begin each day by reading a brief text that highlights some aspect of devotional life in the Wesleyan tradition. The reading is intended to center and focus you in a rich, but limited, aspect of the spiritual life. It will normally reveal some insight from Wesley, but its primary purpose is to enrich your walk with God. As you read each day's text, be constantly reading through or beyond it. Put yourself into the material; do not read it merely as the witness of a Christian who lived more than two hundred years ago.

Following each day's reading, various exercises will guide you to personal reflection. This is closely akin to biblical meditation that ruminates and "walks around" a text until a particular "God word" emerges. The reflection exercises are designed to help you answer the question, What is God saying to me through what I have just read? Do not force this. Do not try to make something happen. Reflection is not magic or automatic. On some days, the personal "God word" will not surface. That is okay. In fact, if you try too hard to find it, it will only elude you more. Relax. Accept the absence when it occurs. It too is part of the formative process. True spiritual formation says, "God's word, at God's time, in God's way."

On most days, however, the reflection phase will yield some meaningful impression. It may be an idea or an emotion; it does not matter. It may emerge rather complete in itself, or it might appear quite unformed and fragmentary;

either way is all right. The time for recording is at hand, and this is the third step on your daily path in the workbook. One writer has called a journal or workbook a "blessing catcher." That is the point of the reflection phase. It provides you the means to store the impression so that it is not lost. At a later time you can reflect further on the impression.

Some people record in prose, others in poetry. Still others will draw a picture or write out a personal conversation with God. Styles to record your impression are many. Use what works best for you. Be creative and experiment with new ways of recording. You may find along the way that you have some fresh ways to reflect and record your experiences with God. Recording is simply the phase in which the insights (the "God word") are captured and considered.

The final phase is relating. It reminds us that we do not come to any moment with God empty handed. We always have something worthwhile to share. The relating phase occurs in two ways in this workbook. First, each day's exercises will lead you to relate what you have just experienced with some previous discovery. Think of it like adding links to a chain. Each day's emphasis is part of a larger picture and progression. By relating your present discovery to your past experiences, you allow the Holy Spirit to unify and harmonize your spiritual growth. You allow God to set your experience in its proper, larger context of formation and maturation.

The second aspect of relating is the weekly group meeting. You do not have to form a group to use this workbook, but I hope you will. John Wesley called this "Christian Conference." He believed God uses community and interaction to instruct us in ways that would not occur if we kept things to ourselves. At the end of each week, a guide for the group is suggested. Use it as a tool to help you, not as a tether to restrict you. Obviously, I have no way of knowing how God may have worked in your life or the lives of the group members. Honor what is happening in the group so that the dynamic presence of the spirit is not lost. At the same time, do not discount the group guide. Some groups allow too much open discussion and the result is meandering, freewheeling, and domination by people who talk too much! Pay attention to the "How to Have a Good Group" section that follows.

By reading, reflecting, recording, and relating I believe you will find this seven-week process to be formative. It will be an occasion for positive spiritual training that will strengthen your desire and ability to approach all of life as devotional. This workbook will come alive when it enables you to make Wesley's teachings a way of life more than a course of study. God bless you as you seek that above everything else!

How to Have a Good Group

Group experiences vary widely. Because they are a means of grace, we want to make them as positive and open to the spirit as we can. The following items are meant to help you do that. If you have not led or been part of a small group before, these guidelines are especially important. For all of us, however, they are valuable reminders of things that help groups go well.

First, take the attitude that you want to learn from others. None of us join groups to impose our views or tastes on others. We come to contribute, to learn, and to grow. Mutual edification is a mark of healthy groups. A spirit of humility should characterize each member. We are all students in Christ's school. We want to experience personal enrichment, and we want to have the sense that the group as a whole is growing.

Second, do not talk too much. No one person should

dominate the discussion. Everyone should be encouraged to contribute ideas and experiences. There are no right comments and no experts in healthy groups. Rather, the spirit inspires and informs through the totality of input. A good group is like a puzzle with each piece adding to the overall picture.

Third, be open to discussing any ideas. Vital groups open people's minds and hearts. No one can completely predict what will become important for a group to explore. This does not mean that a group should chase random ideas all over the place, but it does mean that the group is open and respectful of anyone's need to relate the group process to some significant aspect in his or her life. This may even include the raising of sensitive or controversial ideas. At such times, it is important to realize that you are not making decisions; you are just talking.

Fourth, do not tell long stories. If your personal study causes you to feel you have something important to contribute to the group when it meets, consider how to share it in a minute or two. People often come to groups excited to share something, but because they have not tempered that excitement, they get lost in their own stories. If the experience is important to share, it is important enough to think about, organize, and prepare to present.

Fifth, negotiate the leadership style for the group. This workbook is designed to allow every person to be a potential leader. The guidelines for weekly group meetings are specific and clear enough for anyone to follow. Nevertheless, no one should feel pressured to lead a group session. Talk openly about how you want to arrange weekly leadership. Your group may be comfortable with one person facilitating (not dominating or defining) the sessions. Or, the group may want shared or rotated leadership. Either way, the group must be clear about this early on so that you do not meet with a "who wants to start us off?" mentality. Someone should come to each group session prepared to launch the group and guide persons through the issues—ones that may be suggested in the workbook or ones that may emerge from the group dynamic.

Finally, be a good steward of time. Believe it or not, unbridled enthusiasm is deadly for group life. It may seem perfectly natural to exceed your time when things are really happening. But to evolve into a group that does not know when to quit is ultimately destructive. The old adage that it is better to end too soon than too late applies to healthy groups. It is better to leave a little hungry than to leave feeling stuffed!

There are more group dynamics than these, but the ones mentioned are essential qualities for a good group experience. These qualities should not be enforced as rules so much as integrated naturally into the atmosphere of weekly group meetings. By actually printing the guidelines in the workbook, every member can see and appreciate them. Leaders can be sensitive to see that they are being observed. Most of all, the Holy Spirit will work in and through vital groups. And as you will discover later on in the workbook, the Wesleyan concept of "Christian Conference" is a significant means of grace.

The Initial Group Meeting

Groups work best when they are formed by people who feel a common need to grow along mutually beneficial lines. You do not have to be well acquainted, but you do need to be unified in hope and purpose. Assuming you have at least one other person (and no more than eight) who shares a desire to use this workbook as a means of spiritual formation, the following ideas are provided to guide your first meeting.

The initial meeting is a time of orientation. Begin by handing out the workbook and browsing through it. You might want to read the introduction together as a means of centering the group. Allow every person to get comfortable with the material. Be alert for any hesitation or anxiety, and invite honest, open discussion about the process you are beginning. Do not dwell on the possibility that some may decide not to participate, but make it clear that any such decision is not interpreted as a lack of spirituality. It is natural to opt out of some things after knowing a little more about them. The initial group meeting may cause some to think, "This is not what I thought it was going to be; I am not sure I should commit to this."

Explain that each week's meeting will last no longer than ninety minutes. Emphasize that part of the covenant is to begin and end on time. This is not a mechanical way to limit the spirit; it is merely a good-faith commitment that honors the other dimensions and responsibilities of life. If group life spills over the time period, assure the members that you will still end on time and determine how best to process the "extra blessings" that are occurring. Just as we keep faith with the time, we also trust God to guide us in knowing how to respond to what is happening in the group.

Rather than lay out a one-size-fits-all group plan, turn to page 36 ("Day Seven: The Group Meeting"). Use this outline for your first discussion as an example of the type of format members can expect each week. This will help members get a feel for where they are headed, as well as have a sense of confidence that the group dynamic is not threatening. As you browse through the session, make clear that any and all comments made in the meeting will be strictly confidential. Ask this question and call for response, "Are you committed to the discipline of confidentiality as part of the group experience?" (If you sense hesitation or if there are questions about this, simply point out that confidentiality is an ancient spiritual discipline that some groups have adopted as part of their covenant and that John Wesley promoted in his group meetings.)

Next, turn to page 21 ("Day One: Man of Challenge"). Walk through this section and explain the process as people familiarize themselves with the material. Ask if the format is clear. Again, give time (without moving too slowly) for everyone to feel at home with what is going on. In most cases, silence, nods, or eye contact will let you know that everyone is in agreement. Explain that Day One begins tomorrow, and Day Six is the day before the group meeting. Day Seven is intended to be a day of rest, reflection, and preparation for the weekly group meeting on that day. Do not get bogged down, but do not rush this orientation either. The goal of the initial meeting is to let people know that the group is safe, the material is friendly, the leadership is nonthreatening, and the process is positive.

Finally, ask each person to write the names of all group members inside the front cover. Use this list as a reminder to pray for one another during the week. If you are the group leader, include your telephone number along with your name, so that people can contact you between meetings. Let the group know that the weekly sessions are not a prayer meeting as such, but that opportunity to share prayer requests will be given—even if there is not enough time for formal prayer. Also make it clear that no one will be expected to share or pray aloud as a condition for group participation. The central purpose is not to learn to pray, but to grow in grace.

This part of the initial meeting should take about thirty minutes. Likely, one hour will be enough for the session. With the remaining half hour, use about fifteen minutes for group members to tell about their happiest moment in the past couple of weeks. When all who wish to speak have done so, sing the "Doxology." Use the final fifteen minutes to allow members to tell briefly their expectations for the group—why they are looking forward to the opportunity of using the workbook privately and meeting corporately. End this time with a prayer of thanksgiving and a request for God's guidance. You might say words such as, "It is good to believe God has brought us together. It is good to anticipate that our meetings will be times of special insight and blessing. It is good to know that as we go, we go in the love of God, in the name of Jesus, and in the fellowship of the Holy Spirit. Amen."

As the group closes, say something like this: "Remember, our next meeting is _____, at ___(place)_____, from _____ to _____. I look forward to seeing you then. Call me if you have any questions."

Week One

John Wesley:
Man of Devotion

Man of Challenge

"O begin! Fix some part of every day for private exercises. . . . Whether you like it or no, read and pray daily. It is for your life; there is no other way: else you will be a trifler all your days."[1] These words of John Wesley, written to one of his itinerant preachers, show the importance of the devotional life. But far beyond his regular, fixed times of devotion kept faithfully for over sixty years is Wesley's challenging example of a total life lived in devotion to God.

Many in the Wesleyan tradition are aware of his long-standing commitment to the devotional life. We know of his practice of early rising, and we may even be familiar with several of the devotional books he read. But often that is the extent of our knowledge. Consequently, Wesley is of little concrete help to us as we wrestle with our own spiritual formation. He serves more as a hero than as a spiritual guide.

This is unfortunate. Wesley's devotional life can be a rich source of inspiration and practical help as we seek our own growth in grace. This workbook is one attempt to connect your spiritual journey with the insights Wesley can provide. In the next seven weeks, you will focus especially on Wesley's teachings and example regarding the means of grace. The "institutional and prudential means of grace," as they were called in Wesley's day, are at the heart of Wesleyan devotional life and traditional spiritual formation. You may know them better as "the spiritual disciplines." By whatever name, they are the attitudes and actions that God sees fit to use as ordinary, normal channels to convey grace and to mature our lives. As you move through this workbook, you will have the opportunity to become more familiar with the means of grace, but more especially to experience the presence and blessing of God through them.

We are not here to venerate John Wesley! He would be the first person to cry out, "Don't do that!" He was well aware of his imperfections and his wavering investment in the means of grace. In fact, he monitored the variations with minute examination. Wesley's challenge is not in the absolute correctness of his actions, but rather in the purity of his intention, which was nothing more nor less than to "love the Lord thy God with all thy heart, and with all thy soul, and with all thy mind" (Matt. 22:37).[2] Wesley's devotional practices were only the activities that enabled him to love God and others. In our desire for spiritual formation, we could have no finer aim!

Reflecting and Recording

1. Go back and read Wesley's quotation that begins today's reading. What part of it strikes you the most? Why do you believe this speaks to you now?

_____

_____

_____

2. What is the significance in the difference between having a devotional time and living a devotional life? Which kind of devotion comes nearer to describing where you are right now?

_____

_____

_____

3. Wesley found his devotional challenge in the two great commandments (Matt. 22:37-40). How do these words challenge you in your spiritual formation?

_____

_____

_____

4. If purity of intention is a key to vital spirituality, what do you really want from your devotional life? What do you really intend to bring to it?

_____

_____

_____

Relating

In the space on the next page, jot down some notes to remind you of when your devotional life was most satisfying. What made it so? Are these things still in place, or do you sense God's challenge to renew your spirituality?

_____

_____

_____

DAY TWO

Man of Realism

When we study Wesley's devotional life, we sense we are following a fellow pilgrim in the faith. Wesley had ups and downs just as we do. His devotional life was not perfect, just as ours is not. He made his share of mistakes as he went along.

One of the most notable errors occurred around 1732. Wesley's devotions took a turn toward extreme self-examination. He was preoccupied with taking his own spiritual pulse. At the back of his devotional diary[3] he devised a system by which he could evaluate his progress, or more accurately, the lack of it. This was done by measuring his spiritual vitality against a set of predetermined questions (for example, "Have I thought or spoken unkindly of another one?"). For each time Wesley failed to live up to a certain question, he put a dot on his chart. At the end of the week, he totaled the dots for each question. His system caused him to focus on his faults. Wesley was practicing defeatist devotionalism!

This should be a warning to us. We can easily to slip into a devotional pattern that accentuates the negative. This is especially true if we already struggle with low self-esteem. This does not mean that every devotional period is pleasant and positive, but Wesley's functional mistake serves to instruct us to avoid any plan that doesn't allow the whole story to be told. Through Wesley's example, and in some devotional systems today, we can see how easy it is to practice the first half of James 5:16, "Confess your faults one to another," but to omit the last half, "and pray for one another, that ye may be healed" (RSV).

We should not ignore the negative areas of our lives. God wants to heal and restore us. We must take sin and failure seriously. But Wesley's example reminds us that we find positive spiritual formation not by amplifying our problems, but by appropriating God's grace. Wesley only used this system for a little over a year. He soon abandoned his failure chart, recognizing it for the problem it was. In our spiritual formation, we also must find a devotional style that accentuates healing grace.

Reflecting and Recording

1. What part of today's reading spoke the most to you? Why do you think this is important?

_____

_____

_____

2. Yesterday you reflected on the significant difference between having a devotional time and living a devotional life.
   Do you see any ways that the larger perspective of a devotional life could have spared Wesley from what he recorded
   on his chart during his devotional times?

   _____

   _____

   _____

Relating

Have you ever gone through a period when what you were
doing in your devotions was not having a positive effect?
What did you do to make a positive resolution? What did you
learn about yourself and/or your devotional style through the
experience?

_____

_____

_____

DAY THREE

Man of Discipline

The fact that Wesley made some mistakes in his devotional life did not prevent him from continuing to cultivate his relationship with God. He knew he had discovered the essential element of the Christian life, and he was determined to see it through. Wesley's resulting witness is remarkable. His daily diary entries indicate that for more than sixty years he faithfully practiced spiritual disciplines. To be sure, he varied the format and content from time to time. He was willing to experiment with new things, but his basic intention to relate to God personally did not waver.

Again, it is necessary to balance this long pattern of faithfulness with a note of realism. Wesley knew dry times just as we do. In fact, he had a symbol in his diary to record what he called the "temper" (fervency) of his prayers and other devotional acts. Many days show that his prayers were cold and indifferent. But he kept at it, knowing they would eventually return to being warm and effectual.

I've heard people say, "Well, I'm not getting much out of my devotions right now, so I'm going to stop for a while until the vitality returns." While I can easily empathize with these persons, I have come to see that this approach can be spiritually devastating. It is in the dry times that we need to remain disciplined and faithful. In fact, true prayer grows out of a sense of the absence of God and our need for God's presence.[4] If we give up in times of dryness and weakness, we will miss the joy of meeting the God who comes to us in our need. And we will fail to gain insight into the causes of our dryness. This will cause us to make the same mistakes again and again.

Wesley addresses this issue and reminds us that we cannot base our devotional life on our emotions. We must center it in our will. It must flow out of our sense of need. We know what is right and we do it. We trust God to supply the appropriate emotions, and we do not panic when they do not appear. Even in the absence of emotion, we trust that God is present and active in our lives. Discipline becomes the method by which our devotional life keeps going through fair weather and foul.

Reflecting and Recording

1. How does Wesley's witness of faithfulness during dry times instruct or inspire you?

_____

_____

_____

2. Have you ever thought about monitoring the fervency of your devotions? What benefits do you see? What problems might be associated with the practice?

_____

_____

_____

Relating

Think of other areas in your life where you keep on going even when positive emotions are absent. How do you do this? Why do you do this? In the space below, write out your coping techniques when you must live without supporting emotions. Also, write down how doing this makes you a better and stronger person.

_____

_____

_____

DAY FOUR

Man of Breadth

Beyond a doubt, Wesley based his devotional life in the scriptures. He once remarked, "My ground is the Bible. Yea, I am a Bible-bigot. I follow it in all things, both great and small."[5] He continually referred to himself as *homo unis libri*—a man of one book. By these words Wesley revealed the touchstone and standard of his faith. Yet, he did not limit himself to the Bible.

His scriptural foundation gave him a place to stand in his quest for spiritual life, but he was then free to search for inspiration through a wide range of devotional traditions and materials. Wesley knew the classics. He drew on Anglican, Puritan, Moravian, Greek Orthodox, and Roman Catholic sources. Consequently, his devotional life had a depth and variety that no single source could have provided. Using the Bible as his focus, Wesley was able to achieve a remarkable and useful synthesis of spiritual input from these various sources.

Here is another important word for us. Too many people limit themselves to one perspective in their devotional lives. More than that, some have settled for a devotional life that is based in what I call "pop spirituality." By that I mean a devotional life that is trendy and limited to the latest books from popular authors. Christians have a great need to discover the wealth of devotional material that spans the centuries.[6] We stand on the shoulders of spiritual giants. Wesley challenges us to break out of a devotional narrowness and listen to the saints of the ages, all the while testing all things by the Bible.

Reflecting and Recording

1. In which of the traditions listed in today's reading have you already found and read inspiring devotional classics?

_____

_____

_____

2. How does the Bible help you evaluate the other devotional
   materials you use?

_____

_____

_____

_____

Relating

How do your personal spiritual formation and devotional
practices connect you with the great cloud of witnesses and
give you a sense that you are participating in something that
is valuable and timeless? Have you had any experiences in
the past when participating in a tradition other than your
own that have brought blessing, insight, and growth?

_____

_____

_____

_____

DAY FIVE

Man of Community

Wesley never allowed his spirituality to deteriorate into privatized religion. Whenever he could, he fellowshipped with others and exchanged insights with them. His diary is filled with references to his reading devotional works to others and discussing implications. Wesley's letters are illustrative documents showing how he guided the spiritual progress of others, as well as how he sought guidance from others.

Wesley's concern for corporate spirituality is most clearly seen in his formation of societies where people could find group support. These groups became the hub of Methodism's life and growth. The late Bishop Gerald Ensley was correct when he observed that Wesley gathered believers through his preaching and nurtured them through the societies.[7] Wesley's preaching was much more nearly aimed at awakening persons to their need of God and bringing them to the place of repentance. His development of societies was where the lifelong process of disciple making occurred.

It was through the societies also where Wesley demonstrated the social dimensions of spiritual formation. He never believed that true devotion could ever remain individualized or internal to the group itself. Authentic spirituality thrusts one into mission and into the life of social holiness. Wesley's prayers were among the chief means used by God to show him that the world was his parish. His actions through the societies were the logical outworkings of genuine devotion and testimonies to the corporate nature of the devotional life.

Reflecting and Recording

1. What challenges did you receive through the preceding reading?

_____

_____

_____

2. Why is social holiness a good witness to the reality of personal holiness?

_____

_____

_____

Relating

Have you ever become part of a group that combined nurture and service? If so, use the space on the next page to write down the benefits of being in a group like that. Do you have any sense that God would want the group using this workbook to combine study and service? Do you know of any projects that would be meaningful for the group to adopt during the weeks you are using this workbook?

_____

_____

_____

Man of the Church

Wesley is too often caricatured as a malcontent just looking for some place to jump ship. One must remember that he never allowed his personal spirituality or the spirituality of the societies to become substitute churches. He found his place in the regular worship of the Church of England, and he intended for the Methodists to remain active in their respective churches. Wesley faithfully observed morning and evening prayers using the *Book of Common Prayer* as his guide. He received the Lord's Supper an average of once every four or five days, usually at an Anglican altar, and he observed the festival and fast days of the Anglican Church. In the finest sense of the word, Wesley was a churchman.

He did not do these things because he believed the Church of England was a pure or perfect church. He did not remain faithful to the Anglican Church because he felt its principles and practices were beyond question. He did not remain an Anglican because everyone in the church believed the way he did. Wesley maintained his churchmanship for one reason: He knew that to be a Christian is to be an active member of the body of Christ. No one can be a Christian in isolation. Wesley's devotional life reminds us that there is no authentic spirituality apart from the church. God has called us to be in fellowship with the rest of the people of God. Our devotional life should motivate us toward that kind of support for one another, not away from it.

Many of us have taken vows to uphold the church with our prayers, presence, gifts, and service. Our devotional life should be a means of strengthening these resolutions, and it should motivate us to find concrete ways to express these vows in our membership. Wesley would tell us to beware of any devotional life that does not enrich our love for the church.

Reflecting and Recording

1. What message do you receive in learning that Wesley remained a faithful member of a church he had serious questions about and one that he felt was flawed in many ways? What does his example say about people who "church hop" today?

_____

_____

_____

2. What is the role of a person who stays within a church where there are problems and imperfections?

_____

_____

_____

Relating

Think carefully about the vows of upholding the church with prayers, presence, gifts, and service and write down how you express those vows through membership in your local church. Is your devotional life enriching these vows and motivating you to deepen your expression of them?

_____

_____

_____

DAY SEVEN

The Group Meeting

This seventh day is intentionally reserved for rest and reflection on the previous six days in the workbook. One of Wesley's devotional practices was to use Saturday evenings to review the previous week and get a bigger picture of his spiritual development. This workbook asks you to do the same thing each seventh day. The day is also designed to enable you to prepare for meaningful participation in the group meeting. If your group meets in the evening of the seventh day, you will have the whole day to review what you have experienced in the workbook. If it meets in the morning or early afternoon, you may need to get up a little earlier on the seventh day to review and prepare. However you do it, you are practicing devotional life in the Wesleyan tradition as you experience the benefits of recollection and preparation.

As you gather for your group meeting, come prepared to use the following suggestions as a guide, but not as a restriction. Whoever leads this session should be sensitive to each group member's need to share some new understanding from the past week's work. The suggestions below are a guide for any week of the study.

1. Have each member ask to tell his or her most meaningful day with the workbook. The leader should begin and set the example for this time of interaction. Tell why the chosen day was meaningful.
2. Now share your most difficult day. Tell what you experienced and why it was so difficult. See if any others in the group share your difficulty, or if there are those who can shed some light on the difficulty.
3. Out of the mix of meaningful and difficult, have all who will share what they believe to be their "God word" for the week. The "God word" is not something magical or unusual. It is simply the impression each person feels to be most personal and important. It may be a word of comfort, counsel, or challenge. Think of it as the cream that rises to the top of milk. Allow time for everyone to share.
4. Close the group session with prayer. Do not expect or demand that everyone pray aloud, in a certain way, or in a certain order. Remember what we said in the introduction: The use of this workbook is not directly connected with a prayer meeting. We want to create a prayer atmosphere,

but we are not here to learn how to pray. The most helpful way to do this is simply to ask if group members have prayer requests. As people respond, encourage each person to write down the requests. Then when all who wish to have expressed requests, call the group to silence asking that every person pray for the requests in their hearts. Silent prayer is an especially appropriate action for a group like this since most of the time will have been spent talking. The holy silence of closing prayer is a good way to "be still and know that God is God."

After the intercessory silence has gone on for a reasonable time, the leader should invite each group member to reflect on his or her impressions from God, asking the Lord to make that new understanding a reality in life. Again, allow a time of silence as each person prays. Conclude by leading the group in prayers of blessing. The leader should call out the name of one person in the group. Have all other group members look at that person and pray in unison, "God, bless _____." Repeat the process for each person. When every person has received a prayer of blessing, the leader may end the session by saying, "Assured of God's blessing in our lives, let us go in peace. Amen."

Notes

1. John Telford, ed., *The Letters of the Rev. John Wesley* (1931; reprint, London: Epworth, 1960), 4:103.
2. Unless otherwise noted, scripture references are taken from John Wesley's *Explanatory Notes Upon the New Testament* (1954; reprint, Naperville, IL: Allenson, 1966).
3. Wesley's personal diary should not be confused with his published journal. The journal appears in his standard works. The

private diary is also available in the new Abindgon (Bicentennial) edition of Wesley's *Works*.

4. Theodore W. Jennings, *Life as Worship: Prayer and Praise in Jesus' Name* (Grand Rapids: Eerdmans, 1982), 25-30.

5. Nehemiah Curnock, ed., *The Journal of the Rev. John Wesley* (1909; reprint, London: Epworth, 1938), 5:169.

6. One good way to explore the historic devotional treasures is through *The Upper Room Devotional Classics* and the accompanying study guide, available from The Upper Room: Upper Room Books, Book Order Dept, P. O. Box 856, Nashville, TN 37202-9719. Or call the toll-free number at 1-800-972-0433.

7. Francis Gerald Ensley, *John Wesley, Evangelist* (Nashville: Abindgon, 1970), 47.

Week Two

Constant Company
with Christ

DAY ONE

All Day Long

We take a giant step forward in Christian devotion when we see it more as a life to be lived than as a time to be observed. Consequently, we can more appropriately speak of a devotional life than a devotional time. When we study Wesley's spirituality, we see this coming through loud and clear. He never divided his life into compartments. For him, the essence of life was spiritual. All of it could properly be called devotional.

In our time Henri Nouwen has expressed the same idea in these words: "If I cannot find God in the middle of my work—where my concerns and worries, pains and joys are—it does not make sense to try to find him in the hours set free at the periphery of my life. If my spiritual life cannot grow and deepen in the midst of my ministry, how will it ever grow in the edges?"[1]

This is a good question for all of us to consider. Many have been taught that devotions are the first moments of the morning and the last minutes of the evening. Devotional booklets are sometimes geared to telling us how to spend these minutes each day. While we may appropriately have a quiet time with God at the beginning and end of the day, we must not see that time as equal to the devotional life or separate from the rest of our day.

John Wesley sought ways to express his spiritual life throughout the day. He found it in what he called the means of grace. These were spiritual disciplines that people used to express their faith and receive God's grace. They were divided into two categories: the instituted means of grace and the prudential means of grace.[2] The instituted means were those disciplines evident in the life and teaching of Jesus. The prudential means were those that had been developed by the church to give further order and expression to the Christian life. Taken together, they enabled a person to live a devotional *life*. The rest of this workbook will concentrate on examining these means of grace and applying them to our lives. Before we turn to the particulars, however, it is important for us to grasp the magnitude of the devotional life.

Reflecting and Recording

1. How does your current practice reflect or fail to reflect the magnitude of devotional life?

_____

_____

_____

2. Does the phrase *means of grace* shed any new light on your understanding of the spiritual disciplines?

_____

_____

_____

3. What is God trying to provide through the devotional life? Why is it important?

_____

_____

_____

Relating

Take a look at the devotional material you are using. In what ways does it invite you to a devotional life?

_____

_____

_____

Day Two

Private and Corporate Prayer

For Wesley, the chief instituted means of grace was prayer. It is not exaggerating to say that he lived to pray and prayed to live. He called prayer "the grand means of drawing near to God."[3] Prayer had this importance because Wesley understood the Christian faith as a life lived in relation to God through Jesus Christ. Prayer was the key to maintaining and enriching that relationship. It was the gift of God to humankind to facilitate and mature the relationship. Furthermore, the absence of prayer was seen by Wesley to be the most common cause of spiritual dryness.[4] Nothing could substitute for prayer in maintaining the spiritual life.

Central to Wesley's prayer life was private prayer. He believed that in private prayer one waited in quietness to receive the blessings of God.[5] Accordingly, he began his day in prayer. Much has been made of Wesley's habit to rise early, normally at 4:30 or 5 A.M. While it is true that he did this for more than fifty years, one must also remember that he usually went to bed no later than 10 P.M. In other words, he was careful to provide for his physical needs (such as sleep) even as he cared for the needs of his soul. The principle lies not so much in the specific hour of rising as it does in the fact that Wesley directed his first thoughts to God. He knew that to fix the mind on God early would create a divine consciousness that would remain with him throughout the day.

In addition to these times alone with God was his practice of corporate prayer. Whenever he could, Wesley joined with other Christians for prayer. This might mean gathering with several friends or fellow travelers before or after breakfast, or it also frequently meant going to a church to pray the "Order for Morning Prayer" in the *Book of Common Prayer*. This was more than merely fulfilling an Anglican obligation; it was his conviction that every means of grace has both its private and public expression. Furthermore, Wesley believed there were insights, experiences, and blessings attainable in a group that do not occur when one is alone. Wesley's prayer life was one of harmony between what he did by himself and what he did with others.

In exploring Wesley's prayer life, one naturally asks how

he spent his time. We must be careful not to look at his specific practices as actions to clone, but rather as illustrations to inspire our own faithfulness and creativity. As we might expect, Wesley was methodical in his prayer life. He used a weekly pattern, with each day given to a particular topic.[6] He used the *Book of Common Prayer* as the basis for his praying, expanding his prayer life through the use of other written prayers he collected from a wide variety of sources. At the same time, he built spontaneity into his praying by inserting parentheses at places where he wanted to move outside the text and pray about related matters in his own words. By using a regular pattern, he was able to touch on those things that meant the most to him. By using written prayers, he was able to keep his prayers focused while still allowing for flexibility.

Wesley also prayed throughout the day. He trained his mind to pray every hour and to measure the degree of his devotion at the same time. His diary is filled with thousands of references to such prayer. (He used the letter "p" to designate when he prayed privately.) These prayers were usually brief, one-sentence ("ejaculatory") prayers. They were Wesley's way of bringing his entire life before God. Remember, Wesley was no recluse. He prayed this way in the normal course of his life. Obviously, he did not withdraw every hour for prayer. Instead, he cultivated the habit internally. He trained himself to be able to be fully attentive to his circumstances while being fully devoted to God in prayer. By this means he practiced the principle of "praying without ceasing" commended by the Apostle Paul in 1 Thess. 5:17.

Wesley concluded his day in prayer. The practice gave him a sense of closure and commitment. Whenever possible, he gathered with others for the "Order of Evening Prayer" in the *Book of Common Prayer*. Later in the evening he used other written prayers (with accompanying spontaneity) as he did in the morning. But the overall purpose was different. He used the morning to prepare for the day and the evening to review the day. He made appropriate confession for any sins committed, and he made heartfelt resolutions for improving his life in the new day that would follow sleep. He ended his evening prayers, as many saints had done before him, by commending his soul to God. He remarked that by doing this, he was able to sleep peacefully nearly all the days of his life.

Wesley prayed privately and corporately. These were the marvelous God moments that gave his life its character and strength. By extending them throughout the day, he reminded himself that every moment is a sacred time with God. In the best sense of the old song, God was never more than "a prayer away!"

Reflecting and Recording

1. What principles strike you as most important in today's reading?

_____

_____

_____

2. What practices of Wesley could you modify in your own prayer life that would make prayer more relational and comprehensive?

_____

_____

_____

Relating

Frank Laubach spoke and wrote about "flash prayers." These are essentially the same as Wesley's hourly prayers. What experience have you had with this kind of praying? How has it affected your overall prayer life? If this is a new thought for you, use the remaining days of this week to see how many ways you can utilize brief prayers as you go through the day.

_____

_____

_____

DAY THREE

Spoken and Silent

Wesley prayed audibly and meditatively. He prayed aloud, alone, and in groups. Once again, the *Book of Common Prayer* served him well in such praying, as did numerous other devotional manuals and prayer books. His diary shows that he also often enjoyed combining verbal prayer with hymn singing. Like others before him, he considered hymnody to be a form of prayer. He believed that the spirit of piety and the spirit of poetry were closely connected, and that hymns were a "means of raising or quickening the spirit of devotion."[7] Whether spoken or sung, audible prayer enabled Wesley to converse with God in a real voice, complete with the emotions and intonations that accompany praying aloud. When in a group, such prayer obviously allowed the participants to pray in ways that involved them in each other's praying.

But Wesley also knew the value of silence. His diary reveals that much of his praying was done through his inner voice. Mental prayer gave him the freedom to pray at all times and in all circumstances. It was the secret of his ability to practice hourly devotion. A look at the devotional classics that he read shows that Wesley was familiar with meditative and contemplative prayer. Through his use of silent prayer, he enjoyed deep communion with God—a lifting up of his heart and a pouring out of his soul. Furthermore, silent prayer was a protection against hypocritical praying—that is, praying to be seen and heard by others. Jesus had condemned this kind of prayer, and Wesley wanted to protect himself from it as well. Silent prayer saved him from this error.

Taken together, spoken and silent prayer further illustrate the variety of praying that is open to us. Like Wesley, we can know the freedom of praying either way. On the one hand, we can know the joy of praying aloud even when we are alone. And on the other, we can experience the liberty of praying silently even when others in a group are speaking their prayers. We are not bound to use any particular type of prayer in any given setting. On the contrary, we are free in prayer to express our heart's desire in the most meaningful way for us at any given time.

Reflecting and Recording

1. Which type of prayer is your preference? Why?

_____

_____

_____

2. What kind of devotional material have you found useful in teaching you and assisting you in your preference?

_____

_____

_____

3. What do you feel you need to learn about the other kind of prayer?

_____

_____

_____

Relating

Recall times in your life when you have prayed aloud when you were alone, and times when you have prayed silently when you were in a group. How did you feel when doing this? What have you learned as a result?

_____

_____

_____

Covering All the Bases

Wesley expressed the full range of prayer. He praised, confessed, gave thanks, interceded for others, and prayed for himself. As he practiced these types of prayers, he also expressed the full range of emotions: joy, sorrow, compassion, concern, trust, confusion, anxiety, and so forth. One of the most striking features of his praying was honesty. Often Wesley bared his soul before God in doubts, questions, and cries of anguish.

One of the most moving examples occurred in Georgia when he discovered that Sophie Hopkey had decided to marry another man. Wesley had procrastinated in his decision whether or not to ask Sophie to marry him. Feeling she had waited long enough, she accepted another's proposal. When Wesley learned the news, he went into his garden noting that he attempted to pray. But he could not! In that moment God seemed beyond reach, and he did not try to cover up the feeling with pious, artificial words. Instead, he poured out his heart to God in words revealing the depth of his anguish.

Consequently, Wesley's prayers have the ring of reality. When he prays with warmth and affection, we can know he is being genuine. Likewise, when he records that his prayers are cold and indifferent, we can identify with him. In both dimensions we have a realistic guide. From him we learn that no emotion is off limits in prayer. From him we discover the availability and importance of prayer in all situations. Wesley's prayers reflect the sentiment of the psalmist, "If I ascend to heaven, you are there; if I make my bed in Sheol, you are there" (139:8).

Reflecting and Recording

1. Think about the ACTS prayer pattern (adoration, confession, thanksgiving, and supplication). What aspects of life does each type of prayer enable you to touch and relate to?

_____

_____

_____

2. As you look at your total prayer life, which of the elements in the ACTS pattern do you find yourself using most? Are there any that have not received proper emphasis or expression?

_____

_____

_____

Relating

Have you ever had a time in your life when, like Wesley, you could not pray? Why were you unable to pray? Are you able to pray about that circumstance now? How did you come to the

place where you can pray about it? Or, if you are still unable
to pray about it, why is this so?

_____

_____

_____

DAY FIVE

Student of Prayer

If ever there were a student of prayer, it was John Wesley. He
read hundreds and hundreds of prayers, studied them carefully, and even used them in his own praying. He collected the
prayers of others much like some people collect stamps today.
Sometimes he copied the entire prayer. At other times he
abridged the prayer, capturing a particular part that was especially meaningful to him.

Wesley collected the prayers of well-known persons such
as Jeremy Taylor or William Law. But he was just as likely to
include the prayers of anonymous Christians or those of his
own friends and colleagues. Regardless of the source, Wesley
used the insights from others to advance his own spiritual
life. When people came to him seeking help in their prayer
lives, Wesley usually shared these prayers with them. In fact,

his first publication was *A Collection of Forms of Prayer for Every Day in the Week* (1733), which was a shorter version of the prayers he had been collecting and using for seven or eight years. In their published form, this collection also reflected the weekly pattern of prayers that he used and commended to others.

Here is another important principle for us today. We need to become familiar with the devotional classics, especially with the prayers of the saints. When we do so, we find that we are not alone in our spiritual pilgrimage. Others have shared similar victories and defeats. They have asked our questions, felt our pains, and experienced our blessings. Furthermore, the way they pray is a pattern for our learning how to pray. In effect, Wesley is teaching us that if we will study good prayers, noting their language and subject matter, we will be well on the way to learning how to pray well.

Reflecting and Recording

1. Do you have any books of prayers? If so, use them for a time in order to see what you can learn in studying and using the prayers of others as a guide for your own praying.

2. How do you feel about the idea of a weekly cycle in your prayers? How might this make your prayer list more manageable?

_____

_____

_____

Relating

G. Ernest Thomas used the prayers of others as a means of encouraging people to overcome their fear of praying in a group. At every meeting he would have books of prayers available. For those not yet comfortable praying in their own words, he would ask them to select a prayer from one of the books. When their time to pray came, they simply read the selected prayer aloud. Thomas noted that these prayers were not only meaningful in their own right, but they also became bridges over which hesitant people could walk to begin praying in a group. Why not follow Thomas' example in your group for a while, not only to encourage the timid, but also as an experiment to see how the prayers of others can indeed enrich and inform your praying?

_____

_____

_____

Day Six

God Can Be Known

Perhaps more than anything else, Wesley's prayer life confirms that God can be known. To be sure, we will never plumb the depths of God or understand all God's ways. We will always experience mystery and wonder, but they are balanced with encounter and communion, which Wesley sought and found in his prayer life. He would wish the same for us today.

In his *Explanatory Notes Upon the New Testament*, Wesley provided extended commentary on the Lord's Prayer. Lifting up the phrase "Our Father," he noted that God's presence is in heaven, but not there exclusively, seeing that God fills the earth as well.[8] One of the greatest truths in all the world is that God has taken initiative to reach out to us. We call it revelation. Prayer is our response to God's self-disclosure. We can say with C. Austin Miles, "He walks with me, and he talks with me, and he tells me I am his own; and the joy we share as we tarry there, none other has ever known."

Prayer is not intended to be some kind of complex labor. God wills it to be joyous interplay between our spirit and the Holy Spirit. God is not hiding, even though sometimes we have difficulty discerning the divine presence. God is a person in the sense of possessing qualities of personality that we have as human beings, and God can be known. Prayer is the wonderful gift that enables us to know God. Wesley's life and his record of it in diaries, journals, and letters (to say nothing of sermons and other publications) is a sixty-six year testimony to Jeremiah's promise, "When you search for me, you will find me; if you seek me with all your heart, I will let you find me, says the Lord" (Jer. 29:13-14).

Reflecting and Recording

1. How have you come to know God through prayer? How does your own prayer experience parallel that of Wesley's?

———————————————————————

———————————————————————

———————————————————————

2. What experiences in prayer have you had that would enable you to say, "He walks with me, and he talks with me. . . ."?

_____

_____

_____

Relating

Think back in your life, perhaps even to your childhood. Have you known people who lived prayer-saturated lives? What qualities do you remember about them? What characteristics would you like to exemplify in your own life so that others might one day remember you and your life of prayer?

_____

_____

_____

DAY SEVEN

The Group Meeting

Here you are two weeks down the road in your exploration of Wesleyan spirituality and your growth through it. How is it

going? If you are like me, you may find that some days have
been better than others—that the experience has been some-
what uneven. You may have even skipped some days and had
to play catch up. Don't be discouraged! The goal of this experience is not perfect performance, but conscientious attention
to those things that will produce growth in your life.

As you prepare for the group meeting, don't worry that
you will have to report on any particular accomplishments.
Relax and let your mind and heart roam over the past two
weeks. Allow the Holy Spirit to highlight those portions of your
experience that will enable you to share positively and produc-
tively. Others are doing the same, and God will meet you when
you gather together. To use Wesley's words, you are a covenant
group committed to "watching over one another in love."

Remember, the suggestions for the first group meeting
can be followed in any of the subsequent meetings. In fact,
open sharing of our best and difficult days is frequently all
that is necessary to make the group session meaningful. In
addition to this general pattern, however, consider these additional possibilities for today's session—remembering that
you are under no pressure to cover all the ideas mentioned.

1. Open your time with the leader offering a brief prayer of
   thanksgiving for the opportunity of being together. God has
   already been gracious in making it possible for you to be
   present. Celebrate that reality and seek God's presence for
   the rest of the meeting.
2. Come to the session with a meaningful prayer passage from the
   Bible. Even though John Wesley is the focus of our study, the
   Bible is the inspired source. Spend time today selecting your
   prayer passage and reflecting on its importance in your life.
3. Bring a meaningful prayer book to the meeting. It may be a
   book of actual prayers or a book about prayer that has in-

spired and informed your journey. Remember, on Day Five we looked at the example of G. Ernest Thomas as he taught people to pray through the reading of meaningful prayers. Perhaps you have a prayer, or the like, that has been important to you. There's nothing like a little show and tell to personalize and make tangible the kind of ideas we've studied this week.

4. Close the session with prayer. In addition to the mixture of spoken and silent prayers, write each person's name on a sheet of paper and then distribute the names around the group. The name you draw can be your silent prayer partner for the third week of your study. Before you leave, pray the Lord's Prayer together.

Notes

1. Henri J.M. Nouwen, *Creative Ministry* (Garden City, NY: Doubleday, 1971), xviii.
2. Thomas Jackson, ed., *The Works of John Wesley* (Grand Rapids: Baker Book House, 1979), 8:322-24. Until the Bicentennial edition of Wesley's *Works* is completed, the Jackson edition remains the historic standard. When possible, I will cite both editions, either as "Jackson" or as "Bicentennial."
3. Telford, *Letters*, 4:90.
4. Jackson, *Works* 6:81 and Bicentennial, *Works* 2:209. Sermon: "The Wilderness State."
5. Jackson, *Works* 5:192 and Bicentennial, *Works* 1:386. Sermon: "The Means of Grace."
6. Jackson, *Works* 11:203-37. His "Collection of Forms of Prayer for Every Day in the Week" was Wesley's first publication (1733) and illustrates the importance he gave to this weekly pattern.
7. Bicentennial, Works 7:75. *The Preface to A Collection of Hymns for the Use of the People Called Methodist* (1779).
8. John Wesley, *Explanatory Notes Upon the New Testament* (Naperville, IL: Alex R. Allenson, Inc., 1966), 37. Wesley originally published these Notes in 1755. They have been a doctrinal and devotional standard ever since.

Week Three

The All-Sufficient Word

An Objective Base

The spiritual life must have an objective base. Private revelations must be scrutinized against a recognized and established norm. To put it in biblical language, we must "test the spirits to see whether they are of God" (1 John 4:1, RSV). Failure to do this occasionally results in tragic stories and bizarre acts. Many of us will long remember the 1978 Jonestown incident as a classic example of misguided, maniacal spiritualism. Jim Jones, cult leader of People's Temple, led over 900 persons to commit mass suicide in Jonestown, Guyana.

John Wesley knew that an objective standard was necessary for genuine spirituality. For him, that standard was the Bible. Although Wesley read hundreds of books on a wide range of subjects, he was committed to the centrality and authority of scripture. As stated in Week One, he continually referred to himself as *homo unis libri*—a man of one book. Even though he published approximately six hundred works on various themes, he resolutely maintained that he allowed no rule, whether of faith or practice, other than the Holy Scriptures.[1] In the preface to his *Standard Sermons*, Wesley exclaims, "O give me that Book! At any price, give me the book of God! . . . here is knowledge enough for me."[2]

Wesley confirmed this exclamation with an amazing example of faithfulness to the study of the Bible. For sixty-five years the Bible was his daily companion in the life of faith. It was his primary guide for living the holy life As the heirs of Wesley, we need to make a clear affirmation of the authority of scripture, not as one source among several, but as the norm for Christian thought and conduct. We need to declare that the Bible is the standard by which the results of tradition, reason, and experience are checked.[3] We need to be rooted in the Bible.

Reflecting and Recording

1. In a pluralistic, multireligious age like ours, why is "testing the spirits" a necessary thing to do? How do we go about doing it?

_____

_____

_____

2. Using the Bible as his norm, Wesley integrated the biblical message with tradition, reason, and experience. How does each of these elements enrich our understanding of scripture?

_____

_____

_____

Relating

In the space on the next page, write down an experience in your life when you, like Wesley, have had a profound hunger for the word—a time when you could have exclaimed, "O give me that book!"

_____

_____

_____

Worshipful Reading

We must remember that the primary value of scripture for Wesley was not its serving as some cold, lifeless standard. Rather, he saw the primary value of the Bible in its unique ability to bring men and women into an encounter with Almighty God. Therefore, we recognize that the primary value of scripture is devotional. We need to consider how we approach the Bible, as well as to examine what we find when we open it.

We can learn from Wesley in this regard. We see, for example, that he read the Bible worshipfully. He read the Bible to meet God, hear God, and respond to God. Accordingly, he read in an unhurried, reverent manner. He wrote, "Here then I am, far from the busy ways of men. I sit down alone: only

God is here. In his presence I open, I read his Book; for this end, to find the way to heaven."[4]

To ensure that his Bible study times were unhurried, Wesley chose the early hours of the morning and the quiet hours of the evening. These times allowed him the space to meditate on what he read. His main goal was quality, not quantity. Wesley normally read at least a chapter per sitting, but sometimes he would read only a few verses. His desire was to encounter God, and when he did that, the amount he read was not the most important thing. In this regard, Wesley reminds us that we cannot meaningfully read the Bible on the run. To be alone with God and God's word requires a time all its own and a corresponding attitude of reverence and attention.

Reflecting and Recording

1. Do Wesley's words that he read the Bible "far from the busy ways of men" issue any challenge to you? Do they give you any idea of what that might mean in your life's routine?

_____

_____

_____

2. What insight or guidance do you receive in knowing that the goal of Bible reading is quality, not quantity—encountering God, not just reading about God?

_____

_____

_____

Relating

Is your present method of reading the Bible enabling you to "find the way to heaven"? If so, write below how that is so. If not, use the space below to consider ways you might alter your reading to more nearly achieve this end.

_____

_____

_____

DAY THREE

Systematic Reading

Wesley read the Bible systematically. His usual practice was to follow the table of daily readings in the *Book of Common Prayer*. By using these, he was able to read through the Old Testament once a year and the New Testament several times. This approach also allowed Wesley to read contextually rather than haphazardly. He believed that Christians should know "the whole counsel of God." He exemplified this by reading the Old and New Testaments as well as the Apocrypha.

It would be wrong, however, to suppose that Wesley was

only looking for experience when he read the Bible devotionally. He also wanted to know the word of God. He saw no dichotomy between scholarly study of the Bible and reading for spiritual enrichment. Any new information or insight was further inspiration from God, and he received it as such. Wesley also brought to the reading of scripture a knowledge of the original languages and the best study tools of his day.

Wesley demonstrated his concern for biblical knowledge by preparing the *Explanatory Notes* for the Old and New Testaments.[5] These notes were largely drawn from the writings of others, but they represent Wesley's views on selected texts. He said that he prepared the notes for "plain, unlettered men . . . who . . . reverence and love the Word of God, and have a desire to save their souls."[6] Consequently, the comments are generally devoid of technical, scholarly terminology. But even a casual reading of them shows them to be substantive and beneficial.

Wesley challenges us at the point of systematic reading. Important questions emerge: Am I reading the Bible in a way that brings me in contact with the whole of it? Do I read scripture in large enough portions to see isolated passages in their larger context? Do I use responsible tools to add the insights of others to my own study? Do I have any means of marking, noting, and recording my discoveries? All these points remind us of Wesley's insistence that an in-depth knowledge of scripture requires a systematic approach.

Reflecting and Recording

1. Which of the questions in the preceding paragraph challenges you the most right now? Why?

_____

_____

_____

2. How does your reading of the Bible correspond with Wesley's statement that we should read scripture with "a desire to save our souls?"

_____

_____

_____

Relating

Compare the devotional plan or material you are presently using with the main ideas of today's reading. How does it help you fulfill the Wesleyan principles we've just seen? How can you modify it to make it even more effective? Is it possible that you may need to use other material to better achieve these ends?

_____

_____

_____

Comprehensive Reading

Wesley read the Bible comprehensively. He knew that he had a lifetime to read the Bible, so he did not have to hurry. Nor did he have to be content with a shallow or surface reading. In typical Wesley fashion, he developed a method that provided a comprehensive experience. The main elements of his method are as follows:

1. Dailiness—morning and evening;
2. Singleness of purpose—to know God's will;
3. Correlation—to compare scripture with scripture;
4. Prayerfulness—to receive instruction from the Holy Spirit;
5. Resolution—to put into practice what is learned.[7]

These principles reveal that devotional Bible reading is an experience that touches the whole of life. Wesley was not interested in any form of Bible reading that isolated him from the other experiences of life. These principles enabled him to be present to God, to his own situation, and to those around him.

Reflecting and Recording

1. Which of Wesley's five principles is most alive in your Bible reading right now? How has it enriched your reading of scripture?

_____

_____

_____

2. Which of the five principles is weakest right now? Why? What can you do to incorporate it into your Bible reading?

_____

_____

_____

Relating

In your Bible reading today use the five principles as a guide to further probe and apply your reading of God's word to your life and to your service in the world.

_____

_____

_____

DAY FIVE

Purposeful Reading

Wesley wrote, "Whatever light you receive, should be used to the uttermost, and that immediately."[8] For Wesley, this meant at least two things. First, it meant the personal application of God's word to our lives. Second, it meant that we should seek to teach others what we have learned.

Related to personal application, Wesley encouraged people to pause frequently and examine themselves by what they were reading. We would call this reflective reading. He said that by doing this we would find the Bible "to be indeed the power of God unto present and eternal salvation."[9] This discovery would move us to form appropriate resolutions about the way we will live from day to day.

But purposeful resolutions are never intended to be exclusively private. Full application means that we seek to teach others what we have learned. Wesley put it plainly, "What I thus learn, that I teach."[10] This principle was confirmed many times over in his diary where we see Wesley sharing insights with others as he visited with them. Sometimes this took the form of more formal readings from scripture and other devotional material. At other times, Wesley passed along insights in casual conversation. But always he was open to ways and means of helping others grow in their faith.

A word of caution is in order at this point. Nowhere does Wesley appear to be pushy or dogmatic in his sharing with others. He did not try to make his experience universal or force it on others. Rather, his approach was more sensitive. He allowed the experience of another to be a doorway through which he could share what God had taught him in a similar experience. This approach is in contrast to some today who have "a word from the Lord" for us that must be obeyed or our spirituality is called into question.

Wesley never operated that way. Rather, he shared his insights humbly, knowing that if it were truly a word from God for that person, the Holy Spirit would make the application in the person's life. In this way, Wesley's encounter with God in the Bible serves to remind us that we can relate the events of our lives to the teaching of scripture, and we can be used to help others do the same.

Reflecting and Recording

1. What was the most challenging part of today's reading for you? Why?

_____

_____

_____

2. How have you sought to practice Wesley's principle of personal and full (teaching others your learnings) application in your devotional life?

_____

_____

_____

Relating

In his book *How to Give Away Your Faith*, Paul Little provides seven questions to help us see if we are reading the Bible in ways that will enable us to make it applicable to our lives. As you read the following questions, identify the points you seek readily in your Bible reading and which ideas you need to focus on more diligently: (1) Is there an example for me to follow? (2) Is there a sin for me to avoid? (3) Is there a command for me to obey? (4) Is there a promise for me to claim? (5) What does this passage teach me about God or Jesus Christ? (6) Is there a difficulty for me to explore? (7) Is there something in this passage I should pray about today?

_____

_____

_____

DAY SIX

Corporate Reading

What we have said thus far has dealt primarily with Wesley's use of scripture by individuals. There is a final dimension that completes the picture. Wesley read and used the Bible corporately. He knew there was value for the community of faith to sit under God's word. So in the *General Rules* he required the early Methodists to be faithful in attending services where the word of God was preached and taught. This meant both the Anglican services at the parish churches and the various meetings connected with the Methodist movement: bands, classes, societies, and preaching services. It also meant faithfulness in the reading and explanation of scripture in family devotions.[11]

The corporate use of scripture is further seen in the annual conferences of early Methodism. The *Conference Minutes* are salted with reference to scripture, as Wesley and his followers sought the guidance of scripture in the actions they took. Likewise, the hymns of Methodism were composed with an eye to the Bible. Nearly every line had a scriptural basis. These things remind us that Wesley would encourage the use of the Bible in corporate ways today. He would delight in small groups that form to study scripture. He would urge the church to conduct its business with this question as its guiding light, "What saith the Bible?" Just as he declared himself to be a man of one book, he would want us to be a people of one book.

Reflecting and Recording

1. What are the times and places in which you experience the corporate use of scripture? How do such times enrich your devotional life?

_____

_____

_____

2. In the corporate setting, how important is the role of the leader in his or her knowledge and use of the Bible? What is the role of others in the corporate setting? Why is passive learning unacceptable or even dangerous in the corporate use of scripture?

_____

_____

_____

Relating

If you have a hymnal at home, look up several hymns by Charles Wesley. See how many explicit or implicit references to scripture you can find in them.

_____

_____

_____

DAY SEVEN

The Group Meeting

This week we have made the Bible the focal point in our exploration of the devotional life. In addition to the general suggestions for your group meeting provided for the first week, consider the following as possible ways to use your time together.

1. Bring your personal Bible to the meeting, along with any other translations you find useful. Take turns showing one another these Bibles. There may be some physical things worth sharing, such as the way you underline or record notes in your Bible or the style of your study Bible that enriches your study of scripture.
2. Bring devotional material to the meeting that you are currently using or that you have found meaningful in the past. Again, take turns talking about this material and how it has enabled you to experience a meaningful devotional life.
3. Distribute hymnals to the group. Point out the direct or indirect references to scripture in the hymns you select. Sing the hymns together as part of your corporate worship.

Notes

1. Perhaps the best contemporary presentation of Wesley's perspective (complete with numerous references to his original works) is Thomas Oden's *John Wesley's Scriptural Christianity* (Grand Rapids: Zondervan, 1994), 55-65.
2. Jackson, *Works* 5:3 and Bicentennial, *Works* 1:105.
3. For further reading about the place and significance of the Bible in the Wesleyan tradition see Mack B. Stokes' *The Bible in the Wesleyan Heritage* (Nashville: Abingdon, 1979).
4. Jackson, *Works* 5:3 and Bicentennial, *Works* 105-106.
5. *Explanatory Notes Upon the New Testament* was first published in 1755. *Explanatory Notes Upon the Old Testament* appeared in 1765. The New Testament notes came to stand, along with *Standard Sermons* and *Articles of Religion*, as the doctrinal stands of British and American Methodism.
6. Wesley, *Explanatory Notes Upon the New Testament*, 6.
7. John Wesley, *Explanatory Notes Upon the Old Testament* (Bristol: William Pine, 1765; Salem, OH: Schmul, 1975), 1:viii.
8. Wesley, *Explanatory Notes Upon The Old Testament*, 1:viii.
9. Wesley, *Explanatory Notes Upon the Old Testament*, 1:viii.
10. Jackson, *Works* 5:4 and Bicentennial, *Works* 1:106.
11. Jackson, *Works* 8:269-71.

Week Four

Food for the Journey

Day One

Past and Future

True spirituality always exists in relation to the church. As we have seen, both prayer and Bible study have their corporate expressions. This community dimension of the spiritual life is highlighted even more in the third means of grace, the Lord's Supper. Dr. Albert Outler is correct in stating that Wesley believed the Lord's Supper to be "literally indispensable in the Christian life."[1] Unfortunately, not all of Wesley's followers today feel the same. There is a tremendous need to renew this holy sacrament in our lives and in the church.

Wesley had three main emphases in his theology of the Lord's Supper. We will examine two of them in today's reading and the third tomorrow. All three orbit the questions, What is the Lord's Supper? and What are we participating in when we kneel to receive the juice and bread? Wesley answered first of all that Holy Communion is a memorial meal. When we eat the bread and drink from the cup, we harken back to the act of redemption wrought on our behalf by Christ. Juice and bread are symbols of the New Covenant established by Jesus and are reminders that this covenant is still in effect.

But there is more. We are not merely remembering a historical act that happened nearly two thousand years ago. When Jesus said, "Do this in remembrance of me" (Luke 22:19, RSV), he was using remembrance in the Hebraic sense of recalling an event so thoroughly that it comes alive in the present. This is the sense in which Wesley considered the Lord's Supper a memorial meal. We should remember Christ and our experience of him with such devotion and attention that we relive and renew our experience with him in the present!

Wesley's second emphasis points forward. The Lord's Supper is a pledge of future glory. The sacrament is a promise of the future that awaits the Christian in heaven. Our participation in Holy Communion on earth is a reminder that we will one day feast at the heavenly banquet. In this regard, Wesley saw our reception of the elements as a form of contact with the great cloud of witnesses who have preceded us. The Lord's Supper is a meeting place between the church visible and the church triumphant.

Both these dimensions of the Lord's Supper make it a true celebration. Looking back, we focus on Christ's redemptive work with such passion that we experience his saving grace anew in our lives. Looking forward, we catch a glimpse of the perfect and eternal life that awaits us when this life is over. Our present reception is made alive by what has been and what will be!

Reflecting and Recording

1. Which of these two emphases has been most important in your past participation in the Lord's Supper? Why?

_____

_____

_____

2. What new ideas have you contemplated after today's reading? How can you use these new ideas to prepare yourself to receive the Lord's Supper at your next opportunity?

_____

_____

_____

Relating

As you think back, what is the most meaningful communion service you have ever been a part of? In the space below record some of the details of that experience. What made it so special?

_____

_____

_____

DAY TWO

Christ Truly Present

Wesley believed that Christ is truly present each time we receive the Lord's Supper. This third emphasis places some of us in a new relation to the sacrament. Most of us have some awareness of communion as a memorial meal, and we may have even thought of it as a pledge of future glory. But for many of us, the idea of Christ actually being present is challenging. We must understand what Wesley meant in this aspect of the Lord's Supper.

First, he did not mean transubstantiation. Unlike his Roman Catholic friends, Wesley did not believe there is any actual, material change in the elements. They do not literally become the body and blood of Christ. Second, Wesley did not mean consubstantiation, as his Lutheran friends taught. That is, the bread and wine remaining bread and wine, but Christ actually being present in the elements. He did not believe we had to somehow put Christ into the elements to have him truly present.

Wesley preferred the position of Anglicanism—Christ chooses to come wherever the Lord's Supper is being celebrated. He does not come through the elements, but rather through the spirit. But he is really there! This being so, it is easy to see why the Lord's Supper was such a powerful sacrament for Wesley. Wherever Christ is present, anything can happen. And while Holy Communion is primarily a sacrament to strengthen believers, Wesley also believed it could be an occasion when people were deeply convicted, maybe even converted. He placed no limits on the sacrament's power because he placed no limits on what Christ can do.

This largely explains why Methodists have always practiced open communion. The communion table is Christ's table. The invitation to partake is not reserved for believers, but for any who "truly and earnestly repent of sin. . . ." Outler is again correct when he notes, "It is always *God's* grace, it is never at man's disposal. Thus, it cannot be sequestered by any sacerdotal authority."[2]

Lest Wesley's openness be confused with indifference regarding who partakes, we must remember that he put great emphasis on preparing to receive the Lord's Supper. We will focus on this later in the week, but it needs to be mentioned here. Wesley's openness is rooted in his understanding of grace. Because grace is offered in the sacrament, it can accomplish whatever God desires for the one who receives it. All this is through Christ who comes to us whenever and wherever we celebrate the Lord's Supper.

Reflecting and Recording

1. How are you helped by holding on to the real presence of Christ, without having to believe in transubstantiation or consubstantiation?

_____

_____

_____

2. Does the open table shed further light on the two emphases of communion as a memorial meal and a pledge of future glory?

_____

_____

_____

Relating

Think of how the Lord's Supper might be an occasion for a person to be convicted (prevenient grace), to be converted (justifying grace), or to be further consecrated (sanctifying grace). Have you ever known people who were affected in each way through Holy Communion?

_____

_____

_____

DAY THREE

Unworthy Reception

Communion brings with it certain practical questions and concerns. One of the chief problems has to do with "eating and drinking in an unworthy manner" (1 Cor. 11:27). What does this mean? Misunderstanding this phrase has caused people to refrain from receiving the Lord's Supper. Consequently, Holy Communion is not an integral part of their spiritual formation. This is most unfortunate and unnecessary.

Wesley himself dealt with people like this. He believed that the problem resulted from a gross misreading of Paul's teaching. Whenever anyone said, "I should not receive communion because I am unworthy," Wesley had three basic responses. First, he said that the matter of unworthiness was not related to the person directly, but rather to the manner of reception. Who is ever worthy? The sacrament is precisely for the unworthy, and that is all of us! We are all sinners saved by grace. We approach Holy Communion as a means of grace, because it is grace that we need.

Second, Wesley called people to a close reading of the text. He believed that Paul answered the question. Unworthiness had to do with taking the sacrament in a rude and disorderly way, so that one person was left hungry and someone else became drunk. Partaking unworthily meant doing so in ways that fostered exclusiveness and disunity among the people of God. The problem of unworthiness resides in the way the sacrament is conducted, not in the character of those who partake.

If these two points were not enough to convince a person, Wesley made his third point: We are commanded to partake of the Lord's Supper. Jesus said, "Do this in remembrance of me." He said that Christians desire to obey all the commandments of God. They do not knowingly neglect any of them. The call to obedience is greater than any of the supposed risks regarding unworthiness. Participation in the Lord's Supper is a step of obedience, not a sign of moral perfection.

Does this give us permission to receive communion every single time or under any conceivable circumstance? Not necessarily. There may be times when the spirit reveals that we are living in willful unrepentance. If that is the case, we would do well to remain in our seats and deal with the problem at hand. However, we should never allow a false or unscriptural sense of unworthiness to keep us in our seats. The Lord's Supper is designed for those of us who know how much we need God![3]

Reflecting and Recording

1. Which of Wesley's three points about unworthiness speaks the strongest word to you? Why?

_____

_____

_____

2. How does the traditional invitation in the communion ritual shed further light on the ultimate design of the sacrament?

_____

_____

_____

Relating

Is there anyone you know who needs to hear Wesley's three points and thereby find deliverance from a false and unscriptural sense of unworthiness? Use this moment to pray for that person and for an opportunity to share this good news with him or her.

Day Four

Proper Preparation

We have all had the experience of leaving the communion experience feeling that we had not adequately prepared. Sometimes the way the ritual is conducted makes us feel as if we have had a "herd" experience more than a graced one. The matter of preparation is important, lest we miss the real presence of Christ and his gifts to us.

From what we said yesterday, it's clear that proper preparation begins with a repentant heart. If we have that, we connect with the opening words of the invitation: "You who do truly and earnestly repent of your sins. . . ." This is the pivot on which a decision to partake or abstain ought to be made. No matter what we have thought, said, or done, the table of the Lord is open to us if we are "heartily sorry for these our misdoings."

To know that this is so requires prior self-examination and prayer. Whenever possible, Wesley began to prepare for the Lord's Supper during Thursday evening devotions. He used all the devotional periods from then until Sunday morning to make further preparation. Yet, he knew that such preparation was not always possible, so he wrote that it was not "absolutely necessary."[4] In another place he wrote "that no fitness is required at the time of communicating but a *sense of our state*, of our utter sinfulness and helplessness."[5]

This sense of appropriate need is cultivated by allowing sufficient time for the communicant to get in touch with his or her heart. Published manuals existed in Wesley's day to assist a person in doing that, and as we have said, Wesley normally took six devotional periods preceding communion to properly prepare himself. Furthermore, the worship of both Anglican and Methodist traditions allowed for time in the service for people to cultivate this kind of an attitude. In our day, we should find ways to prepare ourselves, that we might come to God openly and humbly.

Reflecting and Recording

1. How are your preparations for communion like or unlike those of Wesley? What insights did you gain from his example?

_____

_____

_____

2. Do you have any devotional material that helps you prepare for communion? If so, plan to take it with you to this week's group meeting.

Relating

Find out when the next celebration of the Lord's Supper will take place in your church. Follow Wesley's pattern by beginning on Thursday evening to prepare for proper reception. Use your devotional periods on Friday, Saturday, and Sunday morning to continue the preparation. On Sunday, consider going into the sanctuary earlier than usual to bring your preparation to maximum openness to God and to the grace offered you in the Lord's Supper.

_____

_____

_____

DAY FIVE

Frequency of Communion

The rubric for the "Order of Communion" in the *Book of Common Prayer* (1662) stated that "in cathedral and collegiate churches and colleges, where there are many priests and deacons, they shall all receive the Communion with the priest every Sunday at the least."[6] By Wesley's day, this instruction was largely ignored, so that most people received communion only twice a year, others quarterly, and a few monthly. As the frequency of the sacrament declined, so also did its significance in the church and in the lives of its members.

Wesley stood in contrast to this sacramental erosion. He was crystal clear concerning his position, writing that "no man can have any pretense to Christian piety, who does not receive it (not once a month, but) as often as he can."[7] A look at his own diary shows that he averaged taking communion once every four or five days. He urged "frequent" communion, rooting such reception in a spirit of "constant" communion that keeps one's heart perpetually before God. When Methodism became a denomination in North America, he exhorted the clergy to celebrate the Lord's Supper every Sunday.[8]

Once again, Wesley's historic perspective presents us with a contemporary challenge. We have to admit that many churches fail to offer frequent communion, much less weekly communion. The failure to do so is sometimes based in reasons Wesley would never condone, such as an anticipated drop in attendance on Sundays when communion is served. What we must keep in mind, regardless of the actual frequency of offering, is that the Lord's Supper is a means of grace. As such, we do not want to deprive people of the opportunity to draw near to God in this way. If we need to reeducate ourselves in the meaning of the sacrament to see its value, then let us do so. If we must find new and creative ways to make the Lord's Supper available, then let us do so. Holy Communion is at the heart of devotional life in the Wesleyan tradition.

Reflecting and Recording

1. How many times have you received the Lord's Supper in the past year?

_____

_____

_____

2. Are there any attitudes about the Lord's Supper that you
   need to relinquish to more meaningfully partake of this
   sacrament?

_____

_____

_____

Relating

Think of other aspects of your life where frequency of action enriches the meaning of what you're doing. Have you
ever cultivated a love for something by engaging in it regu-
larly? How do insights from other areas of life shed light on
how we might come to find the Lord's Supper more meaningful?

_____

_____

_____

Who Should Receive the Lord's Supper?

We end our week with one of the most practical questions of all. We have already partially answered the question in terms of the condition of our spiritual life and in relation to whether the table should be open to all or just a few. Today we want to focus on the matter of children receiving the sacrament. It is a practical issue that all parents wonder about as their children grow up.

For Wesley, the indispensable prerequisite for receiving communion was baptism. This was not so much his personal opinion as it was the position of the Anglican tradition in which he moved. As a priest in the Church of England, he upheld the church's requirement that one should receive the Lord's Supper only after confirmation, normally between the ages of fourteen and sixteen. However, Wesley was himself an exception to the rule. His father, Samuel, had seen particular spiritual maturity in young John and allowed him to commune when he was nine years old.

Furthermore, Wesley had some misgivings about the rite of confirmation. Taking everything together, he made proven spiritual sensitivity the bottom line for taking communion, not the touch of a bishop's hands. This statement, however, should not obscure the fact that in actual practice Wesley largely followed the custom of the church in administering the Lord's Supper to those who had been confirmed.[9] Admittedly, this leaves us with something of an option, rooting the matter in our perception of our children's individual spiritual sensitivity. We may choose to follow the custom of the church and postpone communion until our children are confirmed (if your denomination has that rite), baptized as believers, or after they make a personal profession of faith.

On the other hand, we may sense in a child particular spiritual sensitivity, and like John's father choose to permit communion at a younger age. If we take this route, then at the very least we should instruct them in the meaning of the Lord's Supper and the significance of what they are doing. As we observe their participation we should have the sense that they have an appropriate appreciation and reverence for the event.

Reflecting and Recording

1. Do you receive from Wesley confusion regarding the answer to today's lead question, or do you receive room to consider the question in terms of your own situation?

_____

_____

_____

2. Why do you suppose Wesley wanted to make baptism a pre-requisite for partaking of the Lord's Supper? Does this point of view connect the two sacraments in a significant way?

_____

_____

_____

Relating

If you grew up in a Christian home, when did your parents allow you to take your first communion? As you recall, was this timely or untimely for you? Why? If you are a parent, how have you dealt with this in the lives of your children? If you do not have children of your own, consider asking these questions to a friend who does.

_____

_____

_____

Day Seven

The Group Meeting

This has been a challenging week for a number of reasons. We have encountered a number of important questions about the Lord's Supper, and we have sought some answers or at least some new information to help clarify our understanding of and participation in the Lord's Supper. Even if you disagree with Wesley's particular views, do not miss the point of the week: the Lord's Supper is a significant means of grace and an indispensable part of the devotional life.

As you approach this week's group meeting, I hope you will gather the insights you have gained in ways that will help you share the larger point. Do not get bogged down in discussing your disagreements. If those are serious or substantial, you might want to set aside some additional time with the group leader. We do not want to ignore our struggles, but we do want the group meeting to be a time to fruitfully discuss the role, power, and place of the Lord's Supper in the devotional life.

In addition to the general suggestions provided for the first week, plan to conclude your group meeting this week with the Lord's Supper. If you do not have an ordained clergyperson as a member of your study group, invite one to come and administer the sacrament to your group. It would be a shame to study all week about the Lord's Supper and not receive it!

Notes

1. Albert Outler, *John Wesley* (New York: Oxford University Press, 1964), 333.
2. Outler, *John Wesley*, 33.
3. For a fuller treatment on each of these emphases, read Wesley's sermon, "The Duty of Constant Communion"; Jackson, *Works* 7:147-157, Bicentennial, *Works* 3:428-439.
4. Jackson, *Works* 7:149 and Bicentennial, *Works* 3:430.
5. Jackson, *Works* 1:280 and Bicentennial, *Works* 19:159.
6. Quoted in Outler, *John Wesley*, 415.
7. Jackson, *Works* 7:156 and Bicentennial, *Works* 3:439.
8. As Lester Ruth has correctly pointed out in an unpublished paper, this does not mean that all Methodists received communion each week, seeing that they often had no elder present to serve it. Rather, Wesley's exhortation is more directed to clergy, urging them not to omit the sacrament in their regular Sunday service.
9. The best presentation of Wesley's complex position on this matter can be found in Frank Baker's *John Wesley and the Church of England* (Nashville: Abingdon, 1970), 157, 236, 244, and 331.

Week Five

Hunger for Righteousness

The Importance of Fasting

In the history of Christian spirituality, the theme of self-denial is of major importance. Saints of the ages have recognized that the spiritual life is not only concerned with what we take on, but also with what we give up. In the rhythm of receiving and giving we find the balance of the spiritual life. In the Wesleyan tradition, the element of self-denial is most visibly represented in the means of grace we call *fasting*.

Wesley stands in the larger Roman Catholic/Anglican tradition by including fasting in the list of the primary instituted means of grace. He joined with those who believed fasting was fully established in the church and practiced by Christ himself. That was sufficient to warrant its use in the early Methodist movement. If grace had flowed through this discipline to Christians in the past, he was persuaded it could continue to do the same in his day.

Wesley's advocacy of fasting was not without the knowledge that it had been abused over the centuries, sometimes expressing itself in rather bizarre ways. He wrote, "Of all the means of grace there is scarce any concerning which men have run into greater extremes, than that of . . . religious fasting."[1] His own life, particularly during the Holy Club and Georgia periods, was a case in point. During these years

(1730-37), he sometimes fasted to the point of breaking his physical health. But extremes notwithstanding, Wesley believed the practice of fasting was a definite aid in spiritual growth.

Reflecting and Recording

1. Wesley stood within the Roman Catholic/Anglican tradition with respect to fasting. What background do you have regarding fasting?

_____

_____

_____

2. Wesley practiced fasting to an extreme at times. Do you know of extreme or unusual practices regarding fasting?

_____

_____

_____

Relating

As you prepare to study fasting this week, what are the major questions you have about it? What experience do you have of it in your own life?

_____

_____

_____

The Nature of Fasting

Wesley's most systematic treatment of fasting appears in his seventh discourse on the Sermon on the Mount. This sermon was included in the Standard Sermons, which gives heightened doctrinal significance to what he said in that message.[2] We will use this sermon to reflect on the nature of fasting in the Wesleyan tradition.

Wesley recognized that the fundamental definition for fasting in the Bible is to abstain from food. He also realized that the Bible describes practices that accompanied fasting that had no necessary connection with it. He termed such things "indifferent circumstances" and sought to instruct the early Methodists in the specific discipline of fasting without additional trappings.

Wesley was also aware that the periods of fasting varied widely in scripture, going all the way up to forty days and nights. But again, he wanted to teach the Methodists about the normal and regular uses of the discipline, not its exceptional expressions. He believed the most common practice of fasting was for one day, from morning until evening. He found support for this in the Bible and in the tradition of the early church. He knew that previous Christians had observed fixed fast days, usually Wednesday and Friday, and that they added other stated fast days throughout the year. As the

Methodist movement grew, he likewise called for Wednesday and Friday fast days (eventually reduced to Friday only), with additional days added during the Christian and calendar year.

The weekly fast days were a reminder that abstinence is intended to be an ongoing feature of the spiritual life. Those who fasted denied themselves so they could give priority to the things of the spirit. Additional fast days corresponded to special seasons, like Lent, when the emphasis was on renunciation. Finally, there were times of particular crisis or need when Wesley would call the Methodists to focused times of prayer and fasting, as a means of yielding to God's will and a means of discerning God's guidance. In all these ways, Wesley was bearing witness to the comprehensive value of fasting in one's spiritual formation.

Reflecting and Recording

1. Consider each of the seasons of the Christian year: Advent, Christmas, Epiphany, Lent, Easter, and Pentecost. Normally we think about what each season tells us about receiving. Consider what each season asks us to give up and what role fasting might play in bearing further witness to our self-denial.

_____

_____

_____

2. What might the practice of weekly fasting do for you in the development of your spiritual life?

_____

_____

_____

Relating

Like many other Christians, Wesley understood that fasting was not meant to be an end in itself. Whatever we give up is intended to provide space in our lives so that we can add something of greater value. What might fasting enable you to receive into your life at this time?

_____

_____

_____

DAY THREE

Types of Fasting

Wesley recognized several types of fasting. The most common was not eating any food at all during the prescribed fast. Take note, however, that he left open the use of some liquid during a fast, especially if the person were ill on a prescribed fast day. But he also recognized the proper place and use of an absolute fast in which neither food nor liquid would be taken.

The second type of fasting was abstinence. Wesley felt it was appropriate when, for health reasons, one could not fast entirely. Here again was another useful form of fasting for those who were sick. Wesley wanted to make sure that persons did not do anything to damage their physical health. Thus persons on an abstinence fast would refrain from all foods except those necessary for the preservation of their health. Although Wesley could not find any specific example of this kind of fasting in the Bible, he wrote, "neither can I condemn it; for the Scripture does not. It may have its use, and receive a blessing from God."[3] The third type of fasting was abstaining from pleasant food. This kind of fasting was used in scripture by those who did not want to defile themselves with sumptuous fare.

An important principle emerges at this point. Wesley made a conscious break with a portion of the Christian tradition that had emphasized bodily mortification in fasting. Although in his earlier days he too had used fasting to "discipline the flesh," he came to see that this was not the central purpose of fasting. He stood against any use of fasting that sought to prove spirituality by extremes in physical asceticism. He wrote, "Yea, the body may sometimes be afflicted too much, so as to be unfit for the works of our calling. This also we are diligently to guard against; for we ought to preserve our health, as a good gift of God."[4]

Wesley believed that when one approached fasting sanely and with the biblical perspective, it could be a very beneficial discipline. It could be well used by those who were under conviction, by those who were aware of intemperance in food or drink, and by those who wanted to find additional times for prayer.[5] In fact, it was the connection between prayer and fasting that Wesley most wanted to emphasize in the devotional life. Because of this, believers could devote themselves to regular fast days, not waiting for either the period fast days of the church or some crisis to lead them to fasting.

Reflecting and Recording

1. What benefit do you receive in knowing there is more than one way to practice fasting?

_____

_____

_____

2. What do you think Wesley would say to a diabetic about fasting? Why is this linkage between physical health and fasting important?

_____

_____

_____

Relating

In our day Richard Foster has suggested that if the main purpose in fasting is to concentrate on God, we may need to fast from other things than food. He suggests such things as television and the telephone. How does this expanded version of fasting invite you to personal and creative growth? Is there anything besides food from which you need to fast?

_____

_____

_____

DAY FOUR

Wesley's Personal Example

As we seek to develop spiritual disciplines we need to look carefully at whose example we follow, and we must not feel compelled to follow another's practices in every detail. I have come to believe that John Wesley offers us a positive and realistic example regarding fasting, complete with a touch of humor in the matter!

For the most part, he followed the custom of the Anglican

Church which encouraged fasting on Fridays, during the forty days of Lent, on the Ember Days, and on the Rogation Days.[6] Between 1725 and 1738 when Wesley was conscientiously patterning his practices after the early church, he observed Wednesday and Friday as fast days. After 1738, however, he seems to have returned to weekly fasting on Friday. In short, Wesley was a good churchman, and he exhorted the early Methodists to be the same.

Using Friday as an example, we can reconstruct the main features of Wesley's fasting. He began his fast following the evening meal on Thursday. This was related to a pattern of devotion related to Christ's passion. By initiating fasting on Thursday night, he was connecting with Christ's experience in the Garden of Gethsemane. This was also the time when Wesley began to make special preparations to receive Holy Communion on Sunday, again a means of connecting with Christ's resurrection.

Usually, he did not eat again until Friday afternoon when he broke fast with tea. Here is where I see a touch of humor in Wesley's example, even though he might not have seen it himself. By breaking fast with tea on Friday afternoon he did not miss a single tea time during the week. After all, God may ask a Britisher to fast from some things, but never from tea! Returning to the more serious and plausible note, by ending his fast on Friday afternoon he was finishing his fast at the time when the Lord cried out, "It is finished!" He was using fasting as a means of participating in the grand story of redemption.

In this overall example we must not forget that Wesley would take liquid during his regular fasting if it was necessary for his health. In his diary we can see occasions when he drank water, tea, or broth during the time of fasting. This further highlighted his conviction that the main purpose of fasting was not abstinence, and surely not mortification, but rather the consecration of additional time to be particularly devoted to God in prayer. The impressiveness of Wesley's example is not so much in the details of each period of fasting as in the regularity and continuity of it. The fact is, he practiced weekly fasting for more than sixty-five years! With that kind of time redeemed for additional prayer and devotion, we can better see why fasting is a true means of grace.

Reflecting and Recording

1. What insights come in recognizing that Wesley followed the example and instruction of his church in matters of fasting? What role does tradition have in shaping our spiritual lives?

_____

_____

_____

2. Was it a new thought for you to discover that Wesley's example was related to Christ's passion? What light does this shed on other connections we might make between our spiritual formation and the life of Christ?

_____

_____

_____

Relating

If you know someone who is an Episcopalian, ask to see a copy of the *Book of Common Prayer*. Examine what it instructs believers to do with respect to fasting today. See how contemporary guidance relates to biblical and Wesleyan perspectives.

DAY FIVE

Early Methodist Fasting

Fasting finds its place in Methodism from the very beginning. In the *General Rules* of 1743, Wesley encouraged the United Societies to practice fasting as one example of "attending upon all the ordinances of God."[7] The *General Rules* lay down no specific instructions as to the time, frequency, nature, or duration of the fast. But very early in the movement, Friday became the regular Methodist fast day.

In 1744, when Wesley held the first annual conference, he addressed the subject of fasting in a way that sheds light on his custom and that of the early Methodist people. He wrote, "[God] led all of you to it, when you first set out. How often do you fast now? Every Friday? In what degree? I purpose generally to eat only vegetables on Friday, and to take only toast and water in the mornings."[8]

These instructions seem to indicate that Wesley was practicing abstinence more than total fasting during this period and that he was recommending the same to his preachers at the conference. Here is yet another example of Wesley's avoidance of rigorous asceticism and his emphasis on the primacy of prayer and devotion during one's fast.

In 1768, Wesley issued a directive to the societies fixing quarterly fast days in September, January, April, and July. Additionally, the annual conference checked up on the practices of Friday fasting. Interestingly, the subject of fasting led into the larger topic of Christian perfection. The conference recorded that the issue of self-denial was significant in the pursuit of holiness, and that fasting was an assistance in that regard. Wesley also believed that God blessed the act of fasting by providing great revival among the people.

We can conclude our brief survey of early Methodist fasting by letting one of Wesley's early followers tell us about her example. Hannah Ball's testimony is typical of many others in the movement. She wrote that her weekly fast day was "a fast day to my body, but a feast day to my soul." She went on to speak of her fasts as a time of "unusual freedom of spirit and communion with God."[9]

We cannot to end today's reading without recalling the clear note of celebration in the fasts of early Methodists, indeed, in Wesley's own example and instruction. We too easily think of fasting as a negative spiritual discipline. Our predecessors considered it a positive act. This difference in viewpoint is a call to reconnect with our tradition and to rediscover the joy of fasting in the devotional life.

Reflecting and Recording

1. Think about the obvious connection between fasting and feasting. The early Methodists saw them as two parts of a larger whole. How might these elements work together in your life?

_____

_____

_____

2. List as many aspects of celebration as you can in relation to
   a regular practice of fasting.

_____

_____

_____

Relating

One of the ancient spiritual disciplines is simplicity. While it
is not one of the formal instituted or prudential means of
grace, simplicity is related to the practice of fasting. How
might fasting enable you to live a more simple life? How
might such simplicity become a means of helping others?

_____

_____

_____

DAY SIX

Fasting Today

This has been a rich week. Starting with the Bible and moving into the examples of Wesley and the early Methodists, we have received a great invitation—the opportunity to take a means of grace that many consider to be negative and to transform it into a wonderful experience. I suspect if Wesley could say anything to us this week, it would be for us to see the delight of fasting, not merely the deprivation. Like all other spiritual disciplines, if fasting is a true means of grace, it is a doorway to liberty, not a hurdle of legalism. We can easily see this as we summarize some of the main lessons we have learned.

First and foremost, fasting is an act that glorifies God by providing additional time for prayer. When I think of the thousands of hours redeemed for devotion by Wesley and the early Methodists, I am humbled in the paltry way I set aside such times for God. I am also stirred to think of the potential that such additional times might hold for the cultivation of my spiritual life.

Second, fasting is an act that reminds us that the spirit is to take priority over the flesh. We are not dualists. That is, we do not abuse the flesh in order to elevate the spirit, but through fasting we are reminded that devotion to God is more important than addiction to the material. Fasting has a way of showing us how much we are attached to self-indulgence. It holds the potential of teaching us that life can be lived more simply and temperately. Fasting is a means of grace that helps us keep the material and spiritual dimensions of life in better balance.

Fasting reminds us that we should engage in anything that affords greater glory to God. In a culture addicted to consumerism, the example of self-denial is still noteworthy. Fasting challenges us to take another look at life's priorities. It also witnesses to others that having, gaining, and satisfying are not the primary goals of life. If we align ourselves with the perspectives we have seen this week, we may also be among those who believe that fasting might now, as then, be an act God would bless with personal renewal and corporate revival.

Reflecting and Recording

1. Have any of your notions of fasting changed as a result of exploring it this week? If so, write down the ones most important to you.

_____

_____

_____

2. What ideas do you have for restoring fasting to the whole church? What might your group, class, or congregation do to renew fasting among the people?

_____

_____

_____

Relating

Since fasting has been a neglected spiritual discipline, perhaps the best act of relating would be to commit yourself to further study of this topic. Begin with the Bible and explore Old and New Testament passages where fasting is mentioned. Then move to books such as Richard Foster's *Celebration of Discipline*, David Smith's *Fasting: A Neglected Discipline*, or Arthur Wallis' *God's Chosen Fast*. Your local bookdealer will be able to suggest other titles to assist you.

DAY SEVEN

The Group Meeting

Perhaps no better way could be spent this day in preparation for your group meeting than actually fasting. Plan to abstain from at least one meal today, using the time in additional prayer. As you do this, meditate especially on how God might want you to incorporate fasting into your continuing devotional life. Listen a lot in your prayer time today. Be attentive to the guidance that God may provide as you fast and further seek God's face.

During the group meeting, invite everyone to talk about his or her most meaningful day in the workbook, the most meaningful insight of the week, or both. Let the tone be as personal as can be. The goal of today's meeting should be the renewal of a neglected discipline. Do not be overly analytical. Seek to catch the spirit of celebration and potential that characterized the fasting of our predecessors in the faith.

Also, devote some of your discussion to the matter of reviving fasting in the church. If your pastor is not meeting with your group, you might set a time to meet with him or her to discuss the corporate dimensions of fasting. Let today's group meeting be primarily a time to consider options. You do not need to nail anything down right now. Let the group be open to the spirit's leading as you envision how fasting might become a continuing means of grace in your group, class, or church. In relation to this discussion, think how the practice of fasting could become a means of stewardship and service to others.

Before you adjourn, consider setting a common fast day for the next two weeks of your group's journey in this workbook. By doing this, you may allow these two upcoming days to be a springboard for the continuation of fasting after your study of the workbook is over.

In addition to whatever other praying you do, allow time in prayer for each person in the group to complete this prayer sentence: "God, I thank you for teaching me that fasting is_____."

Notes

1. Wesley, *Notes Upon the New Testament*, 39.
2. Jackson, *Works* 5:344-360 and Bicentennial, *Works* 1:592-611.
3. Jackson, *Works* 5:346 and Bicentennial, *Works* 1:595.
4. Jackson, *Works* 5:359 and Bicentennial, *Works* 1:609.
5. Jackson, *Works* 5:348-51 and Bicentennial, Works 1:597-600.
6. Frank Baker, ed. *The Works of John Wesley* (New York: Oxford University Press, 1975), 11:79. Unit editor for Volume 11 was

Gerald Cragg. This volume now finds its place within the Bicentennial Edition, although it still carries the Oxford University rather than the Abingdon Press imprint. Ember Days refer to the Wednesdays, Fridays, and Saturdays after the First Sunday in Lent, Lent, the Day of Pentecost, Holy Cross Day, and December 13. Rogation Days are traditionally observed on Monday, Tuesday, and Wednesday before Ascension Day.

7. John Wesley, *The Nature, Design, and General Rules of the United Societies in London, Bristol, Kingswood and Newcastle Upon Tyne*, (Newcastle-Upon-Tyne: Printed by John Gooding, on the Side, 1743), 8. This early document is reprinted in Jackson, *Works* 8:269-271 and Bicentennial, *Works* 9:69-73.

8. "Conference Minutes of 1744," *Publications of the Wesley Historical Society*, No. 1 (London: C.H. Kelly, 1896), 17.

9. John Parker, ed. *Memoirs of Miss Hannah Ball of High Wycombe* (London: Mason, 1839), 39-40.

Week Six

Life Together

DAY ONE

The Mandate

My two greatest concerns about spiritual formation are that it will be perceived largely as a private matter and that it will fail to achieve the outward dimensions God intends it to have. Ours is a very self-indulgent society. A quick stroll through the "self-help" section of a bookstore will confirm the emphasis upon ourselves. We are bombarded with it, including some Christian works and products that do little more than cater to our fallen consumerism.

However, no one can develop a mature spirituality alone, and no one can claim vital spiritual life apart from service in the world in Jesus' name. That is why the last two weeks of our study are so challenging. That is why devotional life in the Wesleyan tradition is so exciting. Long ago, John Wesley (and Christians before him in the Anglo-Catholic tradition) recognized that the means of grace create community and mission. This week we will explore the fifth instituted means of grace, "Christian Conference," the means to community.

The term is not a familiar one today, even though the idea of small-group ministry is well known. "Christian Conference" was the all-encompassing term Wesley used to describe any form of corporate life, including what occurred in the United Societies and the larger church. He urged Christians to gather together to confer about inward and outward holiness. He saw the principle exemplified in the Old Testament emphasis on the people of God, tabernacle, and temple. He saw it further confirmed in the New Testament through Jesus' calling together of the disciples and the eventual establishment of the church itself. The seventeen centuries that preceded him were likewise salted with numerous examples of life together.

Wesley was a devoted churchman. His focus was on the United Societies, which along with other similar societies in his day functioned as little churches within the larger church. Before we explore the United Societies in detail, we must emphasize that Wesley never saw them as substitute churches or groups of Christians operating independently of the body of Christ. But due to the malaise of the churches in his day, Wesley saw the need for places where people could gather for nurture, study, encouragement, stewardship, witness, and service. Infrequent worship alone (as it had come to be expressed in eighteenth-century England) was not producing people devoted to holy living. The United Societies were means to recover what was missing, with the aim of revitalized persons returning to the larger church to be agents of renewal.

That same spirit is needed in the church today. It is reflected in this workbook and the series in which it stands. Mainline denominational decline is an accepted fact. We continue to need little churches within the larger church where people can be renewed and become agents of renewal.

Reflecting and Recording

1. What evidences of self-indulgence do you see in the church today? How might "Christian Conference" help alleviate this problem?

_____

_____

_____

2. Of the key elements of group life mentioned above (nurture, study, and so forth), which strikes you as most important? Why?

_____

_____

_____

Relating

If you have been part of a small group in the past, recall what the most positive aspects and personal benefits were. In what ways did the group enable you to live a more authentic Christian life in the world?

_____

_____

_____

DAY TWO

The Societies

Today we begin an examination of the major components of the early Methodist movement. The largest unit of fellowship (outside of the organized church) was the society. In places like Bristol and London the membership ran into the hundreds. Elsewhere there might be far fewer than a hundred. Between 1739 and 1743, the societies operated more or less independently, although Wesley's personal supervision assured consistency in the various groups. By 1743 it was obvious that some system was needed to coordinate the activities of the societies. So Wesley composed a kind of charter entitled the "General Rules of the United Societies."

Membership in the societies was open to any person who desired "to flee from the wrath to come." In this way, the society served as a means to connect with the prevenient grace of God at work in a person's life, awakening and convicting. The society met weekly with prayer, exhortation, and mutual care being the chief components of common life. The ultimate goal was to help members work out their own salvation.[1] But it is important to note that this was no ingrown spirituality, for the societies also had a clear commitment to stewardship and ministry.

Wesley's motives in establishing the society structure have been variously interpreted. The dominant one seems to have been the realization that immediate nurture is needed for those who have been won by preaching. Going further, Wesley made it clear that preaching alone could not produce a mature spirituality. In the first year of the United Societies (1743) he wrote, "I determine, by the grace of God, not to strike one stroke in any place where I cannot follow the blow."[2] Twenty years later he visited an area where society meetings were in decline and afterward wrote,

> I was more convinced than ever that the preaching like an Apostle, without joining together those that are awakened and training them up in the ways of God, is only begetting children for the murderer. How much preaching there has been for these twenty years all over Pembrokeshire! But no *regular societies*, no discipline, no order or connection. And the consequence is, that nine in ten of the once-awakened are now faster asleep than ever.[3]

Related to nurture was the motive of renewal. Wesley had been influenced at Oxford in the 1730's by a work first published in 1680, *The Country Parson's Advice to His Parishioners*. In it the author declared,

> If the good men of the Church will unite together in the several parts of the kingdom, disposing themselves into friendly societies, and engaging each other . . . in all good Christian ways, it will be the most effectual means for restoring our decaying Christianity to its primitive life and vigor. [4]

By 1743, a number of these religious societies had been formed by Wesley.[5] His use of this form of group experience shows a similarity of spirit with those before him for the renewal of the church.

Reflecting and Recording

1. Why is it important to have a place for people who may only be under the influence of prevenient grace—that is, who have not yet professed faith in Christ, but are only at the stage of awakening and conviction?

_____

_____

_____

2. Where in your church do you have such a place?

_____

_____

_____

Relating

If you are familiar with the contemporary recovery group movements and/or the new worship form called a Seekers' Service, think of how these ministries are an expression of the society movement Wesley used in early Methodism. How do these new ministries contribute to spiritual formation and church renewal?

_____

_____

_____

DAY THREE

Class Meetings

Perhaps better known than any other feature of early Methodism is the class meeting. In many ways it was the heart of Wesley's structure for spiritual formation. As the societies increased in size, he saw the need for an intermediate forum to provide for the continuation of personal nurture—a place where the awakened might be converted. Just as the society reflected prevenient grace, the class meeting came to represent justifying grace. It was in class meetings where the majority of respondents to Wesley's preaching actually became Christians.

In the beginning the class meetings tended to be rather formal, with the leader standing before the group asking questions about the spiritual condition of each member. However, as time passed, the style became more relaxed and a family atmosphere prevailed. Leslie Church describes a typical class meeting in these words:

> Problems were submitted and often solved, spiritual experiences were shared, and the members rejoiced in the conscious assurance of the presence of God. The meetings began and ended with a hymn and prayer, and there was simplicity and intimacy about the act of worship which any formalities would have destroyed.[6]

Besides fellowship, the class meeting also provided the basis for early Methodist stewardship and mission. "A penny a week and a shilling a quarter" became the rule.[7] Across the United Societies, this added up to a considerable sum, and the moneys were primarily used to aid the poor and to support traveling Methodist preachers.

The element of discipline is another noteworthy feature of the class meetings. Each member was given a class ticket that bore the person's name, the date, and the signature of Wesley or one of his preachers. The ticket was good for a quarter, and unfaithful members did not get their tickets renewed for the next quarter. Beyond the tickets, Wesley exercised further discipline through his periodic visits. At these he examined, regulated, and even purged the classes.[8]

By today's standards these practices may seem harsh, but it would be a mistake to read any unloving or legalistic spirit into Wesley's practices. He was loved by his people too much for that, and they seemed to largely understand what he was doing. He was convinced that there could be no spiritual maturity without discipline. And besides, the classes were voluntary associations. No one was forced to attend. Wesley expected those who did attend to obey the rules, not because they were compelled to, but because they chose to. This explains why Wesley could purge the classes as necessary. He threw no one out. Members put themselves out by failing to observe the standards they had previously accepted. Readmittance was always possible and vigorously encouraged.

Reflecting and Recording

1. As you read the description of the class meeting, what aspect of it strikes you as most important? Why?

_____

_____

_____

2. How do you feel about accountability (including possible expulsion) that presupposes a voluntary association and up front agreement to keep covenant with the rest of the group?

_____

_____

_____

Relating

Avail yourself of two excellent small-group expressions: Covenant Discipleship (Box 851, Nashville, TN 37202) and ReNOVARE (8 Inverness Drive East, Suite 102, Englewood, CO 80112). Write each ministry and ask for descriptive materials. When you receive them, compare them with elements in Wesley's class meeting.

DAY FOUR

Band Meetings

For many in the Wesleyan tradition, the bands are unknown features. Nevertheless, we need to include them in our exploration of early Methodist spirituality. Wesley borrowed the idea from the Moravians, although such groups can be traced to a time even earlier.[9] They served as the primary structure for mediating sanctifying grace through particular attention to those who were poised to "go on to perfection."

Wesley utilized the band meetings in his first societies, but by the time of his death in 1792, many bands no longer functioned. Their purposes had been combined with the class meeting. We give attention to the bands because of the underlying principle that gave rise to them. Wesley believed that spiritual formation was fostered as persons of the same gender met in small groups of five to eight members. In the bands men met with men and women met with women to confer in matters of the spiritual life.

Rules for the bands were drawn up by Wesley in 1738, five years before the "General Rules of the United Societies." An examination of these rules indicates that the purpose of the weekly band meeting was for testimony and mutual examination. After prayer and a hymn, one person began the process of speaking the state of his or her soul. Then the rest, in order, spoke concerning their state. Particular attention was given to overcoming personal faults and achieving a sense of forgiveness and peace with God.

Because of the intensive nature of the band meeting, this was the only level in Methodism where members had to be professing Christians. Psychologically and theologically this is not difficult to understand. Wesley knew that intimate, even risky sharing can only be done when one has settled the fundamental issue of being accepted by God. For one just outside the camp, or marginally related to the movement, the band experience could have been too threatening. Furthermore, the band meeting was also voluntary, and statistics indicate that only about twenty percent of Methodists took advantage of this spiritual formation structure.[10]

Before we leave our exploration of the societies, classes, and bands, we need to emphasize once more how the structures of early Methodism corresponded to Wesley's theology of grace. In the order of salvation, grace is the dominant theological theme. The dimensions of grace are these: prevenient (awakening), converting, sanctifying, and glorifying (grace for dying). Hovering over all aspects of grace, of course, is the church. But within the church each element in the Methodist community served as a means to emphasize a dimension of grace: societies (prevenient), classes (converting), and bands (sanctifying). This does not mean that the structures were limited to highlighting one type of grace, but it does show that in the structures of early Methodism the full range of God's grace was demonstrated. Methodist life together enabled people to experience the full gospel of grace!

Reflecting and Recording

1. What benefits do you see in Wesley's provision of bands where men could meet with men and women with women? What contemporary options exist in your church for this kind of community?

_____

_____

_____

2. How do the structures of your church conform to or serve as channels for the various dimensions of God's grace?

_____

_____

_____

Relating

In the past decade we have seen the rise of the Christian women's movement, and more recently the Christian men's movement. If you are familiar with either of these movements, compare the early Methodist dimension of bands with what you see happening in contemporary men's and women's groups.

_____

_____

_____

The Rest of the Story

The societies, classes, and bands formed the heart of early Methodist structural nurture, with each aspect highlighting a dimension of grace. But the genius of Methodist spiritual formation is not exhausted by these three forms of community. Today we want to complete our look at corporate nurture as Wesley intended it.

Within the Methodist movement, we find two other groups that Wesley used to enrich the devotional lives of his adherents. The select societies (sometimes called select bands) existed for those who were making special progress in inward and outward holiness. Wesley knew there were always people who were especially open and poised for growth. The select societies enabled such persons to focus on specific devotional life issues and to grow along particularly meaningful lines.

Conversely, there were always those in special need, or those who were in danger of slipping back in their spiritual lives. Penitent bands were available to reclaim such persons before they fell away from Methodism altogether. People were given the opportunity to wrestle with problems, confess coldness, and otherwise work out their own salvation in ways that would rekindle the flame of devotion. Through these two additional groups we see Wesley's concern that both the ready and the reluctant have means for special care.

Working in addition to the groups, we must also mention the love feasts, watch nights, and covenant services in early Methodism that provided less frequent, but meaningful opportunities for corporate formation. Ultimately, however, we must not forget that everything was geared to connect people with the church. Wesley abhorred the idea that Methodism would become a substitute church for anyone, and to his dying day he declared himself to be "a Church of England man." Likewise, he wanted the Methodists to be active members in an organized church of their choice. As a wise spiritual director and as a genuine reformer, Wesley knew that individual experience in any subgroup gets short-circuited unless it finds presence and expression in the larger church. More than being Methodist, Wesley wanted his people to be Christian. Nothing less is devotional life in the Wesleyan tradition.

Reflecting and Recording

1. As you see Wesley's use of select societies and penitent bands, what comparable dimensions do you see in your church for those who are ready and those who are reluctant?

---

2. What special or occasional services does your church have that enable people to further express their faith and be

nurtured in it? Which of these services do you find most meaningful? Why?

_____

_____

_____

Relating

What evidence in your church or community do you see where people are using various subgroups as substitute churches? While recognizing the benefits that groups have in corporate devotional life, what risks or dangers do you see as well? How might you invite people to connect with the church without devaluing their group experience?

_____

_____

_____

DAY SIX

"Christian Conference" Today

In our day there is a need to recover the experience of "Christian Conference" as a true means of grace. Wesley's decisions and designs help us see the value of life together. I agree with those who believe that Methodism lost its heart when these dimensions were abandoned. I further believe we would see a resurgence of vitality if we could rediscover the dynamic of vital community.

At the same time, this cannot mean a return to the eighteenth century or a mere carbon copy of Wesley's methods. We cannot go back to any supposed Golden Age of Christian spirituality. But we can live in the present and enter the future with the knowledge of key principles. Let us explore some of those today as we bring our week of reflection on life together to a close.

First, we see the principle of voluntary association. Corporate spiritual formation works best when interested people associate with one another. Therefore, we should not expect everyone to participate in anything we do. Sometimes people's reasons for not participating are valid and need to be respected. At other times, nonparticipation is a sign of spiritual malaise. Either way, the vitality of corporate nurture is related to voluntary association.

Second, we have noticed the principle of variety. Group size, constituency, and purpose can be different. Corporate devotional life opportunities can exist for those who are simply seekers, and they can range all the way through to those who are most poised to grow in inward and outward holiness. In fact, we would do well not to try to make any single group cover too many bases. Focus and specificity are means to greater growth for those who participate in any given form of nurture. I know of a church that celebrates and supports any group that has at least five persons interested in pursuing a given goal or topic. This kind of variety keeps groups sharp and meaningful.

A third observation of Wesley's method highlights a uniting of group dynamics to ministry concerns. As groups form within the church, they should be challenged to look outside themselves for service projects. These may include local hands-on and financial involvement, as well as a world vision. The principle of groups in ministry is necessary to prevent stagnation, elitism, and an ingrown spirit.

Fourth, we have witnessed the importance of discipline. While avoiding legalism and a false super spirituality on the part of some, we must not fail to provide corporate nurture that challenges and stretches the members. If we connect this principle with that of voluntarism, we can see that calling for a disciplined life is not an imposition, it is an invitation to grow. Such discipline will include the practice of time-honored means of grace, and it may also include particular disciplines that are chosen and appropriate for a certain group. However it takes shape, we must return to the conviction that without discipline the church will never achieve the maturity and power God intends for it to have.

Finally, life together will create vital lay ministry as people move from having a membership mentality to embracing a discipleship mentality. The contemporary church is too reliant on clergy and in desperate need of genuine expressions of the priesthood of all believers. In every congregation there are mature and willing men and women who can be trained for particular service in the church. They can be equipped to become leaders of groups like early Methodist lay leaders were. This would not only relieve clergy of some stress and strain, but it would also enable the church to be what it is intended to be— the body of Christ in which every member is a minister!

In bringing our week of reflection to a close, perhaps the important thing to remember is that Wesley was able to create groups and expand ministry in a way that preserved cooperation. If our proliferation of groups sets up a competitive spirit in the church, we can know for sure that something is wrong. Perhaps it will be a sign of too much overlap among groups, or perhaps it is a sign that people feel pressure to be involved in too many things. Whatever the cause, competitiveness must be eliminated and a sense of cooperation must be developed. Through cooperation the flow of God's grace is enabled to move through the entire church in ways that no single group can provide.

Reflecting and Recording

1. As you think of your own life, which principle of "Christian Conference" seems most important? Why?

_____

_____

_____

2. As you look at your church, which principle seems most important? Why?

_____

_____

_____

Relating

As you conclude the week on life together, review the system of Methodist corporate nurture. Which dimension would you select as a first step in developing a renewed design for corporate devotional life in your church?

_____

_____

_____

DAY SEVEN

The Group Meeting

You may think that having a group meeting about group meetings is a bit strange, but groups need to engage in periodic self-evaluation. You may want to use the general format suggested for the first week as a means of preparing yourself for this week's group meeting.

For the meeting itself, I suggest that you divide your time into two basic sections. First, spend time discussing the relevance of Wesley's structures and principles in your own group. What have you learned that can enrich the life of your group?

Second, consider your answer to the "Relating" question for today. Make a random list of elements that could be valuable in renewing corporate nurture in the life of your church.

Conclude your meeting with prayer, giving special attention to asking God to guide you, your group, and your church into greater expression of the priesthood of all believers. Pray for your pastor (and any other staff you may have) that further development of lay ministry will relieve them of excessive responsibility and stress in attempting to carry out the ministry of the church with inadequate help.

Notes

1. Wesley, *General Rules*, 1. Cf. Jackson, *Works* 8:267 and Bicentennial, *Works* 9:69.
2. Jackson, *Works* 1:416 and Bicentennial, *Works* 19:138.
3. Jackson, *Works* 3:144 and Bicentennial, *Works* 21:424.
4. Samuel Emerick, ed., *Spiritual Renewal for Methodism* (Nashville: Methodist Evangelistic Materials, 1958), 12.
5. One of the best sources to study the societies is John S. Simon's *John Wesley and the Religious Societies* (London: Epworth, 1921).
6. Leslie Church, *More About the Early Methodist People* (London: Epworth, 1949), 236.
7. Howard Snyder, *The Radical Wesley* (Grand Rapids: Zondervan, 1980), 55.
8. Ibid, 57.
9. Martin Schmidt, *John Wesley, A Theological Biography*, 3 vols. (Nashville: Abingdon, 1963), 1:267.
10. Note by Mr. George Stampe, *Proceedings of the Wesley Historical Society*, V, No. 2 (1905), 33–44.

Week Seven

Into the World

The Outflow of Grace

Our study of devotional life in the Wesleyan tradition has focused on the instituted means of grace, those personal and corporate disciplines that establish and maintain the life of God in the human soul. As important and essential as these means were to John Wesley and the early Methodists, we would not likely have had a worldwide movement born by the use of these means alone. Something else needed to happen. And for Wesleyan spirituality, that something was a concern for the practice of the prudential means of grace as well.

Prudential means of grace may be as unfamiliar to you as instituted means was when we began six weeks ago. Basically, Wesley meant that God has given additional means of grace to the church through which it fulfills the social and relational dimensions of the gospel. Prudent Christians will give attention to them as well as to the instituted means. Emphasizing this, Wesley wrote that the instituted means were not the only means of grace given by God, "Surely there are works of mercy, as well as works of piety, which are real means of grace."[1]

For those of you who may have a background in the Roman Catholic Church, you may recall the phrases *works of mercy* and *works of piety*. Without calling attention to it, Wesley was simply drawing from this tradition (as did his native Anglicanism) to offer his people the instituted means of grace (works of piety) and the prudential means of grace (works of mercy), which taken together constitute the full range of the spiritual life: inward and outward holiness, to use Wesley's words.

The prudential means of grace give Wesleyan spirituality its mission and ministry. They saved the United Societies from becoming ingrown and self-sufficient. At the same time, linking the instituted and prudential means of grace enabled Wesley's social ethic to flow from (and be connected to) his individual ethic, thus keeping them part of the same larger whole. The early Methodist union of personal piety and social mercy forged a more effective instrument for God to use than would have been the case if Wesley had kept them separate. The same is true for us today. Holiness of heart and life remain the twin peaks of vital spirituality. Let us to conclude our study with an exploration of the prudential means of grace.

Reflecting and Recording

1. Why was Wesley wise in keeping the instituted and prudential means of grace combined underneath the larger whole of vital spirituality? What happens when they are too widely separated?

_____

_____

_____

2. What creativity do you see in helping people understand the difference in works of piety and works of mercy? Does this wider view invite people of wider interests to claim authentic spirituality? How?

_____

_____

_____

Relating

In a booklet published years ago entitled *Spiritual Dryness*, Walter Trobisch speaks of the danger of Christians becoming spiritually bloated. This condition occurs, he writes, when we become too much engaged in the intake dimensions of the spiritual life and not enough concerned about the outflow. How does this imagery speak to you? How does it help you see Wesley's concern? Have you ever been spiritually bloated?

_____

_____

_____

DAY TWO

Doing No Harm

The first prudential means of grace is *doing no harm*. The social dimension of the spiritual life is expressed in what we do not do, as well as in what we do. This is not a negative ethic as much as it is a displacement ethic. By that I mean—and I believe Wesley did too—that we must first detach ourselves from counterproductive attitudes and actions before we can devote ourselves to those things that are life giving.

At the same time, Wesley was not calling his people to measure their spirituality according to what they did not do. He had seen the destructive effects of stillness (a term in his day that described Christians who became excessively passive), and he knew that you cannot build a positive spirituality on negativism. Nevertheless, he saw that many people must first get away from some things before they can head toward other things. He knew that in the realm of human relations, we must commit ourselves *not* to do some things, as well as to do others. A vital spirituality always asks, What do I need to avoid in my walk toward maturity in Christ?

Doing no harm was not Wesley's attempt to bind Christians. Rather, it was his attempt to chart the boundary lines—to put a frame around the picture of the spiritual life. To be sure, his list of prohibitions includes some "dated" things, and he did not consider his list to be exhaustive.[2] He saw his examples as illustrative of dimensions of living that all serious Christians would avoid. Wesley could not conceive that any Christian would knowingly harm another person, either by speaking or acting against him or her.

Reflecting and Recording

1. What dangers lie in the spiritual life when we put too much emphasis on what we do not do?

_____

_____

_____

2. What dangers lie in the spiritual life when we do not realize that some things have to go if vital spirituality is to come?

_____

_____

_____

Relating

In the "General Rules" Wesley lists examples of things to avoid. If you were to draft a list of things in contemporary living that Christians must not engage in, what would it include? Why is this list important for you? How might you communicate it to others without falling into the trap of legalism or trying to legislate spirituality?

_____

_____

_____

DAY THREE

Doing Good

The real thrust of Wesley's social spirituality was its positive expression doing good. Here too he made a list of examples for the people of his day. He did this under three subcategories. First, he expected Methodists to do good to the bodies of others. This dimension related to such things as food, clothing, shelter, visiting the sick and prisoners, and so forth. Here is precisely why early Methodism was a true relief ministry as we think of it today. The Foundry in London, for example, included a school for girls, a home for widows, a food bank, a clothing store, and a literacy program as well as the full complement of preaching, worship, and small-group expressions.

Second, Wesley wanted the early Methodists to do good to the souls of others. Under this category we can trace the

Wesleyan motivation and methods for evangelism and disciple making. Present also, was Wesley's concern that error be refuted and sound doctrine taught. For our purposes today, we need to see how closely Wesley connected physical relief and spiritual renewal. He felt total liberty to lead with one or the other, depending on the needs of a particular person or group. But he did not consider the job done until the other had been brought alongside.

The third subcategory was doing good especially to those who are of the household of faith. This did not mean that Christians were to exhibit special treatment to other Christians that they would not give to others. But it did mean that Christians should stick together, avoid schism, and abstain from any hurtful practices that would erode their witness in the world. Wesley believed that the Christian community was a kind of laboratory. If believers could not act properly toward those of like mind, it was doubtful they could sustain right attitudes and actions with the world at large. Furthermore, in a world that marginalized Christian faith, Wesley felt the world would love its own. Therefore, Christians should exercise particular sensitivity toward other believers. But whether toward believer or unbeliever, the positive ethic of doing good was to characterize an authentic spiritual life.

Reflecting and Recording

1. The old hymn "Help Somebody To-day" says, "Tho' it be little—a neighborly deed—Help somebody today." How is this an expression of Wesley's ethic of doing good?

---

2. How is your church an expression of a broad range of ministries aimed at doing good? Do any new possibilities come to your mind?

_____

_____

_____

Relating

Once again, considering that Wesley came up with concrete expressions of doing good, what specific expressions would you list that would fulfill each of the three categories: doing good to the bodies of others, to their souls, and to fellow believers? Why are these especially important for you? How can you prevent these from deteriorating into legalism or measurements of spirituality?

_____

_____

_____

DAY FOUR

The Ordinances of God

The third aspect of the prudential means is *attending the ordinances of God*. A look at Wesley's list shows it essentially includes a restatement of what we have called the instituted means of grace. The ordinances of God are essentially the corporate expressions of the instituted means. This is yet another way Wesley wanted to keep the spiritual life as a seamless garment. Just as the instituted means of grace (which promote personal and corporate inward holiness) flow naturally into the prudential means (which promote personal and corporate outward holiness), so the reverse will be true. As we seek to live a life of love and service in the world, we will necessarily see that such a thing is impossible and hypocritical unless there is a corresponding devotion to the authenticity of our own lives.

Wesley was doing two other significant things in urging attendance at the ordinances of God. First, he was grounding his social ethic in those elements that are not subject to cultural and historical adjustment. Specific examples of avoiding evil and doing good might change from one generation to another, but the instituted means of grace are transcultural and transhistorical. As we attend the ordinances of God (through private practice and public observance) we can trust the spirit of God to make specific what we should and should not do. The ordinances of God give social spirituality its roots.

Second, Wesley effectively removed the ability to put things into neat, disconnected categories. He eliminated the idea of any Christian camping out in either inward or outward holiness. This connection rules out being governed by personal preference and creates a stretch in the spiritual life for everyone. For those of us who can get lost in wonder, love, and praise, there is the reminder that a world awaits our witness and service. For those who can get consumed in good works, there is the reminder that rest and renewal are essential for authentic spirituality to make it over the long haul.

The prudential means of grace with their threefold emphasis bring us full circle. They keep the cycle of profession and expression going, just as inhaling and exhaling keep us going. The first reading in this workbook included a quotation about the importance of fixing times for practicing the instituted means. Now, let us allow Wesley to complete the picture by sharing the importance of maintaining the prudential means as well:

> It is impossible for any that have it to conceal the religion of Jesus Christ. This our Lord makes plain beyond all contradiction by a twofold comparison: "Ye are the light of the world. A city set upon an hill cannot be hid." 'Ye' Christians 'are the light of the world' with regard both to your tempers and actions. Your holiness makes you as conspicuous as the sun in the midst of heaven. As ye cannot go out of the world, so neither can you stay in it without appearing to all mankind. . . . So impossible it is to keep our religion from being seen, unless we cast it away. . . . Sure it is, that a secret, unobserved religion cannot be the religion of Jesus Christ. Whatever religion can be concealed is not Christianity.[3]

Reflecting and Recording

1. To what extent is your spiritual life a seamless garment in the sense Wesley preserves it? Where do you need to sew the parts more closely together?

_____

_____

_____

2. Considering the larger picture, do you tend to seek an inward holiness or outward holiness? What invitation from God do you receive in balancing your preference with the other side of the coin?

_____

_____

_____

Relating

If the ordinances of God are fundamentally the public expressions of the instituted means of grace—prayer, searching the scriptures, the Lord's Supper, fasting, and "Christian Conference"—how is each aspect reflected in your corporate participation in the body of Christ?

_____

_____

_____

DAY FIVE

Recovery

The recovery of devotional life in the Wesleyan tradition will not and cannot mean a return to the eighteenth century or a simplistic repetition of early Methodism's actions. There are places where a recovery of specific practices can be done and would be beneficial. But in far more places, what we are calling for is a recovery of the Wesleyan *spirit*. This workbook rests on the premise that we cannot recover the spirit without a clear knowledge of the original (whether in attitude or action). We have not looked back at Wesley and the early Methodists merely to copy them, but rather we have explored their spirituality in order to be challenged by them.

As we spend our final two days in the workbook, it is important to begin to distinguish between return and recovery. We cannot go back to any previous age, but we can enrich our age with the principles and priorities we observe in the Wesleyan tradition. That is what this whole experience has been about, allowing Wesley to speak one more time:

> It is most true that the root of religion lies in the heart, in the inmost soul; that this is the union of the soul with God, the life of God in the soul of man. But if this root be really in the heart it cannot but put forth branches. . . . [through] instances of outward obedience.[4]

Reflecting and Recording

1. Why is it impossible to go back to another time or place? Why is this a danger in developing our devotional life?

_____

_____

_____

2. As you look at your own spiritual formation, how have you maintained the proper distinction between return and recovery? Are there any ways in which you need to make this distinction?

_____

_____

_____

Relating

Go back to the fifth week when we looked at fasting. On the fourth and fifth days we reviewed Wesley's example and that of the early Methodists. We noted that this pattern was related to a weekly devotional scheme that followed the passion of Christ. Why might this be an example of something you could not return to? How can you nevertheless recover the Wesleyan spirit? You may want to consider this in relation to each of the means of grace as well.

_____

_____

_____

DAY SIX

Methodism

Wesley stuck with the name *Methodist* to describe the movement. Implied, of course, is the element of method in one's personal and corporate devotional life. As we have seen in our journey through this workbook, the method revolves around the practice of the instituted and prudential means of grace. Wesley's methodism is not a one-size-fits-all plan. It is, rather, a comprehensive participation in the full range of God's grace. It is holiness of heart and life.

Today, I want you to spend less time reading, and more time reflecting on this one question: To what extent am I a *methodist*? I do not mean a denominational affiliation. I mean the kind of disciple reflected in the pages of this workbook. To what extent does your devotional life reflect the method of true spirituality available to you through the instituted and prudential means of grace?

As you have a miniature silent retreat today, be balanced in your reflection. Give the spirit of God permission to congratulate you where you are doing well. Then allow the spirit to challenge you where you can do better. Most of all, seek to discover the extent to which the kind of devotional life we have explored actually exists in your life right now. Wesley's early Methodists were affiliated with a number of denominations and theological traditions. What united them was a common devotion to God, a common allegiance to Christ, and a common desire to be inwardly and outwardly formed by the spirit. As you bring your study of this workbook to a close and as you anticipate your final group meeting tomorrow, reflect on how those same convictions represent the heartbeat of your spiritual life.

DAY SEVEN

The Group Meeting

To predict or try to guide how this final session will go is almost impossible. By now, you have become acquainted with one another and familiar with the group meeting format. Do not feel that you have to follow any particular format this week, but keep the goal of closure in mind. As possible approaches, I suggest the following options, although I would not expect your group to do them all in one meeting:

1. Have members share their one or two most outstanding experiences during the weeks of using this workbook.
2. Ask if any members have significant struggles that they need to share as a result of using the workbook.
3. Consider options for further group life. I do not mean the

mere continuation of this group, since some may be ready for a break, but I do mean discussing things people might want to do together in the future. Among other options, remember that this workbook is part of a larger ministry provided by The Upper Room. You might want to use other resources in this series or any of the other fine devotional materials which The Upper Room has available.

4. I hope that you will be able to celebrate the Lord's Supper together as you close your final group session. You might also want to consider using the Wesleyan Covenant Service. Ask your pastor or some ordained person to be present to lead you in this act of worship.

5. I also ask you to consider having the leader read this personal message from me to the group:

Even though we have not met, I sense a kinship with you through your use of this workbook. Many times as I have been writing, I have felt close to those who would one day use this material. In a way I have felt close to you. Thank you for allowing me to share things out of the Wesleyan tradition that have become so important to me. I hope they have helped and blessed you. Please pray for me and know that I have prayed for you as this workbook has taken shape. Most of all, may what we have experienced here be used by God to make us more like Christ and enable us to be found faithful in the service of the one who is head over heels in love with each of us. Blessings as you continue the journey!

Steve Harper

Notes

1. Jackson, *Works*, 7:17 and Bicentennial, *Works* 3:385.
2. Jackson, *Works*, 8:270 and Bicentennial, *Works* 9:70-72.
3. Jackson, *Works*, 5:301-2 and Bicentennial, *Works* 1:539-40.
4. Jackson, *Works*, 5:303-4 and Bicentennial, *Works* 1:541-542.